Echoes of Imola

DEDICATION
To Ayrton Senna and Roland Ratzenberger, and all the other racers at
Imola for whom the outer edge of the envelope proved too fragile

Echoes of Imola

DAVID TREMAYNE

Foreword by Professor Sid Watkins

MOTOR RACING PUBLICATIONS LTD
Unit 6, The Pilton Estate, 46 Pitlake, Croydon CRO 3RY, England

First published 1996

British Library Cataloguing in Publication Data

Tremayne, David
  Echoes of Imola
  1.Automobile racing – History
  I. Title
  796.7'2'09

  ISBN 1-899870-05-9

Photoset by JDB Typesetting, Croydon
Printed in Great Britain by
Hartnolls Limited, Bodmin, Cornwall

Contents

Foreword

by Professor Sid Watkins
President, FIA Medical Commission and Expert Advisory Group

This book provides a fascinating and detailed account of the evolution of the Imola racing circuit to its present-day form. The triumphs and the tragedies intrinsic to Grand Prix Formula One racing are described sensitively and intelligently by the author without hysteria or false sentiment.

The story cannot be told without stirring one's emotions, and this was particularly so for me. The events of the weekend of May 1, 1994 at Imola changed the world of motor racing – not only for me, but for millions of people worldwide. The loss of the promising young Ratzenberger and the most accomplished Senna within virtually 24 hours was a devastating and almost terminal blow for Formula One.

The recovery described in this book is a tribute to the resilience of the devoted workforce in Formula One at all levels, and to the intelligent and progressive response – for once – from the FIA. The rapid changes to the cars – though controversial at the time – and the response of the circuits to change configurations and increase safety measures, with more extensive run-off, better gravel beds and a search for better tyres and new forms of barrier, have restored confidence through a period when cynicism and external political pressures bore heavily on the sport and nearly ablated it.

Now, with excellent co-operation between drivers, their spokesman Gerhard Berger and the Expert Advisory Group initiated by Max Mosley, President of the governing body FIA, we can all strive to make motor racing as safe as humanly possible. I have to emphasize that commercial interests have been left aside in the development work already begun in the last year and for the future changes envisaged.

Many people regret, and will continue to criticize bitterly, the changes in configuration of the circuits, but in my view there is no other option save to install much despised chicanes, which destroy both the spectacle and the image. Given a retrospective choice between a *Tamburello* or a Senna, I do not believe any sane person would now select the wall.

Nevertheless, the unexpected will inevitably occur, despite man's best endeavours, and the spectre of severe injury and death will continue to haunt one's waking thoughts, and to poison one's dreams.

ACKNOWLEDGEMENTS

Anyone will tell you, books like this don't just happen, and they certainly don't just flow from one mind. Along the way you pick up information from other people, and conversations or events often prompt thoughts or open up fresh lines of investigation. My thanks are due to the following for their companionship, assistance, information or inspiration, or in some cases all four:

Jean Alesi; Daniele Amaduzzi; Gerhard Berger; Gianni Berti; Herbie Blash; John Blunsden; Martin Brundle; Diana Burnett; Erik Comas; Gerard 'Jabby' Crombac; Andrea de Adamich; Ron Dennis; Frank Dernie; Bernie Ecclestone; Peter Gethin; Franco Gozzi; Patrick Head; Alan Henry; Damon Hill; Tim Holloway; Jeff Hutchinson; Alan Jenkins; Franco Lini; Maureen Mitchell; Steve Nichols; Paul Owens; Riccardo Patrese; Henri Pescarolo; Harvey Postlethwaite; Jo Ramirez; Nigel Roebuck; Nigel Snowdon; John Surtees; Trish Tremayne; Murray Walker; Professor Sid Watkins; Chris Witty; Nigel Wollheim; Tim Wright; plus Rosa and Leo at *La Pergola*; *Autocourse*; *Autosport*; *Motoring News*; Ezio Pirazzini's *L'Autodromo di Ferrari*; and the staff at the *Autodromo Enzo e Dino Ferrari*.

Introduction

Few nationalities embrace their motor racing with quite the same passion as the Italians, nor revere their heroes in quite the same manner or with their depth of respect.

Walk in the paddock at Monza or Imola today, and of course you will find the inevitable Ayrton Senna memorabilia, but you will also still find the Gilles Villeneuve teeshirts, caps and photographs, or even figurines of Tazio Nuvolari, for the Italian fans – the *tifosi* – do not forget. They may invade tracks when their beloved Ferraris do well, but they do it with a style and underlying sentiment that is quite at odds with the yobbish football-hooligan xenophobia that Silverstone had to endure in that debacle at the 1992 British Grand Prix, or the Neanderthal aggression of the new strain of German superfan.

If you turn right out of the main gate at the *Autodromo Enzo e Dino Ferrari* in Imola, and then take another right, you are led round the back of the circuit, along the concrete wall that skirts the Rivazza, through the throng of *tifosi* and their tents, along roads that cherish the memories of past greats. There is something touching in the naming of the Via Ascari, the Via Nuvolari. And even more so of the Via Musso, which accords the same respect to the oft-forgotten young Roman who died at Reims back in 1958 trying so bravely to uphold the honour of Italy and Ferrari in team-mate Mike Hawthorn's wake.

It escapes me who first said those beautiful words: "to die is commonplace, but to have lived in the hearts of men..." But the Italians understand them well. Those heroes who are dead continue to live for them, and through them.

I drove back to our hotel in Fontanelice on the Friday evening of the 1995 San Marino Grand Prix feeling comfortably happy that, against all of our pessimistic expectations, we had come back to Imola. And at one point I stopped my car, to scribble some notes of inspiration for a piece of work the following day. As I leaned on a front wing I looked back across the circuit, and by pure chance the one area visible through the trees was *Tamburello*.

The advertising hoardings said Agip, in giant black letters on a yellow background, and as effectively as curtains round a hospital bed they all but screened the spot where, 12.4 seconds into the seventh lap of the previous year's race, Ayrton Senna's life had come so violently to its end and an era had ended. They dominated the background to the new version of the corner on the circuit named in the honour of the late Enzo Ferrari and his ill-fated son Dino.

A year earlier, *Tamburello* had been a sweeping left-hand bend that seemed to go on forever and which called for maximum speed from even the least competent drivers, yet it was hardly in the same league as Spa's *Eau Rouge* or Mexico City's *Peraltada* when it came to demanding the utmost levels of skill. What it did require most of all was suspension of the knowledge that a concrete wall lay only 14 paces to the right, 'protecting' the drivers from the river that lay behind it.

Now, a year on, *Tamburello*, like Imola itself, was a pale shadow, hacked down from its 190mph glory to become a combination left-right-left corner that at a stroke took away much of the character. *Villeneuve*, the equally steely right-hand sweep that follows and leads to the *Tosa* hairpin, and where Roland Ratzenberger also lost his life that terrible year, had similarly been emasculated. Imola, once one of the world's more distinctive tracks, now appeared on the television screens to be yet another of the new breed of sterile venues so beloved of Formula One's power brokers, whose eyes monitor more the advertising locations rather than the curves that challenge men and machines.

For all that, I was quietly pleased that we had returned, and that Imola had not sunk forever into the mire of history, or gone the same way as those depressing places, Hockenheim and Zolder. Several of us felt the same way. Whatever they do, the German and Belgian tracks will forever live in infamy as the circuits that killed Jimmy Clark and Gilles Villeneuve, however unfair such blunt appraisal might be. Somehow, Imola will be different. You know, for example, that no Italian fan would ever let Senna's memorial spot become so disgustingly littered and abandoned as the Germans have allowed Jimmy's stone to become, as if fresh generations cannot care less about the fallen heroes of yore.

And as I looked out across the rolling green hills, densely packed with trees and vines, and later still as I drove through Codrignano and watched the creeping grey mist signal the onset of evening as it encroached stealthily upon the side of the narrow country road, I felt curiously grateful that Imola had not suffered such a fate. Somehow the beauty of the area and the open emotion and character of its people deserved so much more than to be remembered for those most ghastly reasons: the deaths of one of the sport's greatest ever racers and the quiet Austrian now forever condemned to stand in his shadow.

Twelve months earlier the sport we all love had been plunged into one of its blackest weekends, as something malign that nobody could understand seemed to permeate the paddock in the form of a series of disasters which piled horror upon horror until many were literally stunned by events. It was as if, after years of effort, safety and, perhaps, complacency, the sport had been visited by some terrible pestilence that struck at its very core and threatened everything that so many of us gathered there that weekend, and millions watching around the globe, held to our hearts with passion. It was a cold, cruel reminder that, no matter what we do and think we are doing in the name of safety, the risk will always be total.

And it seemed a tragedy, too, that such a beautiful place might bear such a terrible stigma, for the people of Imola have always loved motor racing. Worse still, that we might never return. As this book progressed I was surprised and heartened to find how many racing people shared that view. Yet as the sport tentatively rebuilt itself with a race that suggested that the cars created in the wake of the accidents held the promise of real excitement, so people gently began to accept Imola once again as a racetrack worthy of affection.

At the spot where Ayrton Senna died there were touching tributes and floral gifts, and so there were a little further down the road, where men such as Roland Ratzenberger's friend Mika Salo had gone, quietly and without fanfare, to pay their respects to him. Little by little, as the 1995 weekend unfolded, so the tension eased and Imola was once again accepted back into the world of Formula One, as if even the hardest hearts understood that it, too, mourned. The fallen were remembered, as they always will be by those with heart, but the arena of their departure merited no further opprobrium. There was something deeply touching in that reacceptance, in which lay a tacit forgiveness of one mighty sin that had threatened to destroy other, warmer, memories of the very fabric of a racetrack steeped in motorsport history.

Our little hotel in Fontanelice, *La Pergola*, is run by Rosa and Leo, two warm, generous hosts who look foward to our annual visits as much as we look forward to making them, and where the home-cooked *tortellini alla penne* and the accompanying Barolo are peerless. On the Monday morning after the 1994 race my colleague Nigel Roebuck and I were packing our cases in the car, each subdued and reflective, when Rosa came to each of us with a bottle of red wine. Her eyes were red-rimmed, and with a few words of broken English she pressed the bottles into our hands and embraced us. It was her way of offering condolences, almost as if to apologize for Imola, and that simple gesture encapsulated everything there is to love about Italy in general and Imola in particular. Rosa understood, as only a true fan of motorsport can understand.

The day after I got home from the 1995 race John Blunsden called me to ask my feelings about Imola, and I told him some of the foregoing. He was sounding me out to see if I was interested in writing about its heritage; he wanted me to put on record images of a circuit whose history – long before that terrible weekend in 1994 – had already been so deeply etched with passion and emotion as to make it unique amongst motor racing venues. Now, in recalling some of that history, I hope I have been able to convey why Imola has such a special place in the hearts of so many of us who regularly follow the Grand Prix scene.

DAVID TREMAYNE
Harrow and Stapleton, 1995

1
The weekend the luck ran out

Part 1 – Rubens

"It's just a bit difficult to breathe because of my nose, and my hand hurts a bit, but otherwise I'm okay. I'm off to play with the nurses now..." – Rubens Barrichello

Looking back more than a year after the events of the 1994 San Marino Grand Prix, the shock and the hurt have receded and been replaced by a resigned acceptance that this was the way Fate intended things to be. Formula One is such a fast-moving beast that at times it can deny the respite people need to cope with and adjust to traumatic situations. It's like being swept along by a floodtide, on a never-ending sea. Such acceptance, psychiatrists would probably tell you, is all part of the healing process, part of taking the first steps to recovery after a tragedy. Yet nobody who was at Imola that fated weekend will ever forget the intensity of their feelings, nor the brutality with which the face of motor racing was so completely changed.

The year had all seemed so clear cut as we had boarded the planes out to Brazil for the first round, only a few weeks earlier. The winter game of musical chairs had finished, and we knew who would be driving, and for whom. And through it all we had known one thing with complete certainty: Ayrton Senna was about to resume his domination of Formula One in the car that, since 1991, had put him on his back foot; the car which, in the hands of his arch-rivals, had forced him more often than not to accept the second best that was so alien to him. In a Williams-Renault, we all thought, he had a score to settle and was simply going to wipe the floor with everyone else. He had 41 wins to Alain Prost's record of 51, and now that he had eased Prost out of the car and out of Formula One altogether, it seemed only a matter of races before he would have a new record tally of victories to go with his record tally of pole positions. Perhaps he would even do it before the year was out.

Damon Hill, a star of 1993, would remain as Senna's partner; at Benetton, the increasingly impressive Michael Schumacher would be joined by JJ Lehto, and we were delighted that the Finn had finally been given a chance to show his true worth. Much was expected of Mika Hakkinen and Martin Brundle in McLarens that were now powered by Peugeot's new V10, while Gerhard Berger and Jean Alesi could be relied on to row their new John Barnard-designed Ferraris along at a reasonable pitch. There were new entries, too, from Pacific and Simtek. The year held great promise.

What none of us could possibly have known, even as we headed for Imola all too aware that Senna had yet to finish a 1994 race and that the upstart Schumacher and his Benetton-Ford had suddenly become the pacemakers, was that the old era was about to be changed irrevocably; that, as surely as the Roman Empire had fallen, so the reign of Senna was soon to come to an end and that tragedy would usher in a completely new era. With Prost retired and Nigel Mansell still in self-imposed exile in America's IndyCar series, Ayrton Senna's death would bring down the curtain on one of the most turbulent – but also one of the greatest – eras of motor racing, and set a fresh stage for the rise and rise of Schumacher and of Benetton.

Because this was Imola, the atmosphere was light in the press room and the paddock as free practice unfolded on Friday. There was a definite feeling that the season was now about to get underway properly and, truth be told, it simply added spice that Ayrton was having to come from behind. Nobody had relished the sort of walkover that his marriage to Williams seemed to presage, but this was different; now he was an underdog for a while, and it was going to be well worth watching his every move to see how well he coped with the sort of pressure from Schumacher that he had once himself applied to Prost. Only the week before, Niki Lauda had voiced the opinion in *Motoring News* that Schumacher was already superior to Senna. It all made great copy, and added to the sense of excitement.

Then, after 16 minutes of official qualifying on Friday afternoon, the mood suddenly changed. We had no way of knowing it then, but the train of catastrophe was already rolling. Coming through the very quick *Variante Bassa*, the right-left flick that leads to the final *Traguardo* corner by the pits, Rubens Barrichello had lost control of his Jordan in the biggest possible way. As it oversteered over the kerb it was instantly launched into the air and at undiminished speed it straddled the tyre wall on the outside of the corner and slammed with horrifying energy into the steel hawser safety fence before bouncing back and somersaulting one and a half times.

This was probably the biggest impact a Formula One car had been subjected to on the track since Martin Donnelly's massive shunt in his Lotus at Jerez in 1990. I had been unfortunate enough to witness that first-hand, and as we watched the television replay of Barrichello's accident, the same immediate concerns for the driver's welfare leapt to mind. The angle at which his head appeared to have impacted with the safety fence did not look good.

As they so often have been at Imola, the medical and rescue services were on the scene literally within seconds – certainly Professor Sid Watkins, the FIA's medical chief, was there from his parking spot just beyond the corner within 15 – and the television revealed that helpers had been in action before the shattered Jordan actually came to rest.

As Barrichello was taken first to the medical centre, then airlifted to the Maggiore Hospital in Bologna, it became apparent that the Brazilian had had a truly miraculous escape. Formula One breathed a collective sigh of relief, and mentally patted itself on the back for the significant progress it had made in safety matters.

Rubens had been knocked out, and for a while afterwards was suffering from retrograde amnesia, which apparently is typical in such incidents. He literally recalled nothing of the crash. There were no lasting effects, and his most serious injuries were a cracked rib and a broken nose, although he sustained some nasty facial cuts where his head hit the side of the cockpit on impact. He was well enough to joke from the medical centre. "I don't know what happened, but I think I was quick! I feel okay – it's just a bit difficult to breathe because of my nose, and my hand hurts a bit, but otherwise I'm okay. I'm off to play with the nurses now and I'll be back tomorrow!"

And he was, but he was in no state to compete, so he travelled home to Cambridge on the Sunday morning. As he did so, Jordan's chief engineer, Gary Anderson, gave his summation of the accident:

"I think the problem was that normally Rubens would attack *after* that corner, as he went into a quick lap. That time he started pushing as he went *into* the *Variante Bassa*, but he hadn't gone hard enough through it up to that point so he didn't really know what to expect. He'd only just done his 'out' lap from the pits. It looked as though he was a little wide turning into the right-hand section, and there may still have been some oil down there from Hakkinen's problem in the morning."

The Finn's McLaren had caught fire there during free practice when an oil pipe became detached, and the humour that had yet to be silenced surfaced as FIA President Max Mosley remarked, upon observing the ball of flame behind the car: "It's his afterburner!"

"The right front wheel came back and brushed his helmet," Anderson continued, "but the real damage was done when his head hit the side of the tub."

A keen diarist, Barrichello told me a few months later: "I'm the kind of person who is sometimes in the middle of nowhere, listening to good music, and suddenly I'll go and write something. To me. I like to do this. It's not a crazy thing. And sometimes you go back, maybe to 1985, and there is something right there that you wrote, and I like it.

"At Imola I wrote that I was 24 hours from my next qualifying, one day before my crash. I was very happy, the weather was nice... I showed this to my father afterwards and said to him: 'Look at this. How bad is it, because 24 hours before I was so happy, and look at me now. Look at my nose...'

"And he said to me: 'Why are you not happy? You're living. You're still here. You could not have been here.'

"His words changed my mind again because I was thinking badly and he pulled me up again. This is the thing I have from him, and that's fantastic."

Later that Friday Senna gave a press conference. In retrospect, his words had the ironic ring of tragedy. "Imola is dangerous," he said. "There are quite a few places which are not right as far as safety is concerned. But," he added in a supremely valid point, "there are other circuits like that..."

And he was asked why the drivers accepted that situation, and why they hadn't bothered to do anything about it. Looking back now it seems incredible that so many people in the sport had allowed things to get to the point that they had reached as far as safety was concerned, but that is the dubious value of hindsight. The simple fact is that everyone seemed to believe that acceptable levels had more or less been reached. It was like the motor racing world prior to April 7, 1968, the day that Jimmy Clark died; the harsh new enlightenment had yet to come, and to bring with it the wave of fresh awareness of safety shortcomings.

Senna shrugged at the question in an eloquent gesture that indicated that he had more pressing matters on his mind than finding yet another fight to get into with authority.

"I am the only World Champion left," he said. "And I have opened my big mouth too often. Over the years I have learned that it is better to keep my head down..."

Part 2 – Roland

"It was not going to make any difference for Roland if I drove or not. But I had to decide if I am prepared still to take risks like this."
– Gerhard Berger

I look on it now as one of those supreme ironies that the first person I saw when I walked into the paddock at Imola on Thursday afternoon was Roland Ratzenberger. A hand grabbed my arm as I passed the Simtek motorhome, and there he was, with that thick mop of tight-packed curly hair, the slow, sing-song voice, and the grin. That big smile that seemed to cut his long face in half hadn't changed over the years. We had first met in 1987 during his assault on the British F3 Championship, and an easy friendship had followed. Roland was one of those fellows who are so open and honest that you liked him instantly. He was as intensely competitive as all the other madmen that you would meet each weekend, but unlike some of them he could take that step back and analyze himself, and admit when he'd screwed-up. I liked him immensely, and so did my elder son Tom, who was coming up for three years old at that time and, with a child's innocence, had instantly christened him Roland Ratzenberger-and-chips-and-beans the moment they were introduced. Roland thought that was highly amusing, and a small boy found one of his first heroes.

Our paths had diverged since 1987, when Roland headed for Japan to make his fortune, and I moved into Formula One to cover races and spend mine. Now here he was, back on the scene, still grinning that lovely grin. He'd already done the races in Brazil and TI Circuit Aida, somewhere up a goat track in Japan, but we'd not bumped into one another properly until now. He asked about the kids and we brought ourselves up to date, and promised to talk longer after qualifying on Saturday, when there would be more time. It was the last time I would speak with him.

The atmosphere in the press room was again lighthearted when second qualifying got underway on Saturday afternoon, as if the air was filled with unspoken celebration that Barrichello had escaped from the Big One with nothing worse than a broken nose. It was another endorsement of the infallibility of the modern Formula One car, such as we had seen with Berger at Imola in 1989, or Warwick at Monza in 1990. Or even Martin Donnelly, despite his horrible injuries, at Jerez later that year.

The day was warm and humid, and appeared to hold the promise of quick times. Schumacher was the first one to come out, lapping his multi-blue Benetton in 1m 21.942s to stay in second place as Pedro Lamy struggled to 1m 25.295s with his recalcitrant Lotus. Then Schumacher did 1m 21.885s, close enough to Senna's Friday best of 1m 21.837s to grab the attention. Others came, too. Hakkinen in the McLaren, then Berger in the brilliant red Ferrari loved by all of Italy. Then Johnny Herbert, who spun his Lotus and entertained everyone by rotating it on the throttle just in front of Christian Fittipaldi's Footwork. Wendlinger, Lehto, Brundle, Larini. Then Hill came out, together with the ripple of expectation that always precedes a driver who might record a quick time: 1m 22.780s, then 1m 22.587s. Good enough for fourth. Then 1m 22.168s, a better time, but not yet quick enough to improve his grid position. The afternoon felt lazy, with the sun beating down outside, and the fans in the press room were trying lamely and not very effectively to disperse the heavy, sluggish air.

And then the television screens were full of an amethyst car rolling to a halt after what had clearly been a big impact, its driver slumped in the cockpit, head lolling. A Simtek, of course. But whose was it? David Brabham's? Ratzenberger's? My notes read: RR, big shunt, knocked out. Red flag. Tosa.

We watched, and bit by bit the reality emerged. Beside me, Timothy Collings, Grand Prix reporter for the *Daily Telegraph* and the Reuters news agency, opened his Tandy 200 almost automatically and his fingers began flying across the keyboard. "What's happening?" he snapped. "Feed me as it goes along." And I began to tell him, scene by scene, what the television screen was showing us. Tim would bash out a paragraph and send it immediately to Reuters, before updating it the next moment. And so it went on, visions transcribed into words, relayed, and then sent round the world. Almost the last visions of a man we had all known and liked. A detached part of me acknowledged and greatly admired Timmy's professionalism that day.

"It's bad, but he should be okay," somebody said. "He's just out for the count."

But Joe Saward, formerly one of *Autosport*'s men and now freelancing for the fated *CarWeek*, had realized the truth. "Look at the helmet," he said quietly. "Look around the eyes."

And where he pointed we saw the colour of blood, and we too knew the truth, absolutely, from that moment. Roland was dead.

Since the Canadian Grand Prix on June 6, 1982, when poor Riccardo Paletti had struck the back of Didier Pironi's stalled Ferrari at the start, nobody had been killed at a Formula One race meeting. Nobody had died in a Formula One car since Elio de Angelis' testing accident in a Brabham at Paul Ricard, four years later. Many had forgotten the real risk. Indeed, some had never been present when death had visited a race track, had never really thought that this sport was any different to the football or tennis on which they had cut their journalistic teeth. They would find their emotions in complete turmoil as the weekend unfolded.

Down at the shattered little Simtek team's motorhome, the vultures were already gathering. Their tragedy was big news. It was easy to be angry and cynical as we watched team owner Nick Wirth come under siege from the national newspapermen and the television crews, but news is the same the world over. Somebody suffers, somebody else digs out and captures the story of their suffering. Somebody else watches it on television, or reads about it in newspapers and magazines, and walks away after experiencing the vicarious thrill, horror and compassion. I'd seen death before at the track, but it's not something you ever want to get used to. This time I was reminded how war correspondents and photographers have to approach their jobs. It was not a time for moral judgments.

Some drivers went out again once qualifying resumed, some didn't.

Senna and Hill, and Schumacher and Lehto did not participate. At Benetton, Tom Walkinshaw summed up the feelings of both top teams when he said: "We think staying in the garage is the right thing to do in the circumstances."

Dinner that evening was a subdued affair, and in particular I felt for Keith Sutton, the photographer, who had been close to Roland over the years. The following day would be worse still for him, for he and Senna had been friends since Ayrton had first come to Britain to race in Formula Ford.

On Saturday, Roland's fellow countryman Gerhard Berger put some things into perspective as he explained how he had anguished about whether to drive the next day, and why he had finally decided that he would. Normally Gerhard is one of the bounciest drivers, always ready with an amusing quip and a quick grin; one of the practical jokers of the sport. But this time his face was set in a hard mask. The accident had doubtless also triggered memories of his own fiery moment at *Tamburello* five years earlier.

"Most of you are gonna ask whether it was right to continue to drive," he began, in that slightly musical style he has. "Honestly, I saw the accident. I saw it in repeat and I know what happened. I know how heavy it was, how bad it was for the driver.

"I already knew before I went out that the situation was critical. But without even knowing, I could feel it myself. It was the first time that I have found myself shaking after an accident. I was sitting in the car, I watched it on the monitor. And when they started to get him out of the car I could see that it was going to be very bad.

"Of course, in our job you are sometimes a bit prepared to see situations like this. But as it was another Austrian driver, as it was a personal contact to another driver, it was even worse. I know that you should not make a difference between a driver that you know and a driver that you don't know. But it affects you in a different way.

"I went out from the car. I felt sick. I went to the motorhome and I was shaking, all my body. Then the difficult situation was coming, to say if I was going to drive or not.

"I told myself that the question was not whether I was going to drive now. The question was whether I would drive tomorrow and in the future, or if I was not going to drive at all. It was not related to this afternoon, it is related to whether you are prepared to have this risk or not. It was not going to make any difference for Roland if I drove or not. But I had to decide if I am prepared still to take risks like this.

"Honestly, yesterday, when Barrichello went off, it gave me a picture of how close sometimes we are between life and death. I saw it today. I was really on the limit. But I said to myself: 'Do you want to race tomorrow or are you not going to race?' And I said I was going to race.

"From this moment on, I told myself to concentrate on the job because it was not going to make any difference to anybody. It was a difficult situation, and it was very hard."

Gerhard's words had even more of a chill about them in retrospect, and there wasn't a man or woman who heard them who wasn't intensely moved by his courage, or the spirit that humanity can muster in times of deep emotional stress.

Simtek, too, decided to race, and Nick Wirth and his colleagues had also been through a night of soul-searching. "No words can convey my personal thoughts on yesterday's event, which robbed the world of a brave and talented driver and fine friend for so many of us," said Wirth. "Roland had dedicated his life to achieving his boyhood ambition of rising to the top in motorsport. We were immensely proud to have given him his debut in Formula One, and for him to lose his life at this stage defies comment.

"Above all else, we want our actions from here on to reflect the enormous respect we had for Roland, and it is for this reason we have decided to race today. We are confident that Roland, always the ultimate competitor, would have wanted us to do so."

In all of this, Ratzenberger's team-mate, David Brabham, quietly bore a massive responsibility as he did everything that he could to help shoulder the burden, and both he and his wife Lisa needed considerable courage to get through the weekend. On the Sunday morning Brabham boosted morale by setting 18th fastest time, and in the race he would run as high as 13th before retiring. "I lost a close friend yesterday," he said with feeling.

Part 3 – Ayrton

"It is going to be a season with lots of accidents. I'd even risk saying that we'll be lucky if something really serious doesn't happen."
– Ayrton Senna

All sorts of stories abounded about Ayrton Senna that weekend, and in time much of his behaviour took on the mystique of legend. Certainly he came to Imola under a lot of pressure to claw back some of the 20-point lead in the World Championship that Schumacher had opened with his two victories. And certainly he was preoccupied at times as he tried to get the best from an aerodynamically modified Williams FW16 that was at last beginning to behave somewhat better than it had in Brazil and Japan. But as if there wasn't enough to worry about on the technical front, there was Barrichello's accident on Friday afternoon to place him under further strain. The two of them had been close ever since the younger Brazilian had gone to him for advice at an early stage of his racing career, and Ayrton had been greatly concerned by Rubens' accident.

"He was the first person I saw when I woke up in the medical centre," Barrichello had said. "All through my career he had given me many kindnesses."

Then came the Ratzenberger tragedy, and again Senna went through torment. At the time of the Donnelly accident in Spain, Senna had been one of the few drivers to visit the Irishman as he was lying on the track, having been torn out of the wreckage of his car, and again in the medical centre. I always felt that there was a partly selfish streak in such behaviour, because the detached Senna wanted to learn as much as he could about every aspect of his craft, even the bad side.

But there was another very important component, too, an intense underlying compassion from a man whose emotions were so often protected behind a hard shell of apparent arrogance. At Imola his immediate impulse, once he had realized the seriousness of the accident, was to secure a ride in a car down to the *Villeneuve* corner, where the accident had started, and on to *Tosa*, where the car eventually came to a halt, to see the situation for himself and judge whether there might be something he could do for Ratzenberger. Tragically, there was not. Then later, he was to come under even more pressure when the stewards sought to sanction him for having done so. According to them, he had had no business being there, a judgment which did them no credit whatsoever. It also demonstrated their singular lack of understanding of the feelings of the sport's foremost driver when confronted with the sort of tragedy which they all fear, even though they try to convince themselves that it will never happen to them.

Senna had predicted a season of accidents following the enforced revisions to the cars' aerodynamic qualities, and in an interview with the German newspaper *Welt am Sonntag*, published on the day of his accident, he had been quoted as saying: "At the weekend my fears were borne out in tragic fashion; Roland Ratzenberger, racing in his first season, died after an accident on the fastest part of the track. The day before, Rubens Barrichello hit a fence at high speed.

"I know from my own experience that as a young driver one goes into a race in a totally different way and accepts risks that you shake your head about later. Our problem is that at this moment there are many young drivers, and that increases the danger."

There was also the situation about the future of safety measures, and at Niki Lauda's probing a number of drivers, principally Senna and Schumacher, but also Berger and Brundle, had agreed to have a meeting in Monte Carlo prior to the Monaco Grand Prix, to see about reviving the dormant Grand Prix Drivers' Association.

And as if all this was not sufficient, there were emotional problems in his private life. Rumours abounded of a blazing argument with his brother Leonardo over Ayrton's girlfriend, the model Adrianne Galisteu. She and Ayrton had been together for a year now, but his family did not approve, and subsequently, in her hastily published book on her time with Ayrton, she would allege that after his death they would try to buy her out of their lives for $2,000. According to some sources, Senna had wept in the spat with his younger brother; later, when he had called Adrianne on the telephone, he had been in a high state and told her that he did not want to race the following day. But then he had calmed down, and when he called her later that evening he seemed to be himself once more, after greater reflection.

He certainly seemed calm enough on raceday morning, and during the course of the warm-up session he sent a message of greeting on the air to his old enemy Alain Prost, who was now commentating for the French TF1 television network. "A special hello to my dear friend Alain – we all miss you," he said, and the use of the adjective was affectionate, not sarcastic. Later, at Renault, they met and embraced, and their feelings for one another appeared, for the first time in a very long while, to be completely genuine. It was a *rapprochement* that was not only long overdue, but which, in conjunction with his Sunday newspaper comments, hinted that the king of the Formula One jungle was feeling just a little exposed to the young cubs without his old rivals Prost and Mansell there to draw some of their fire.

Just before the drivers climbed into their cars, and while he was still in the shelter of the pit garage, Senna asked his chief engineer to place something in the cockpit of his Williams. "Don't let anyone else see it," he urged. It was a furled Austrian flag, which he had intended to wave in victory as his tribute to Ratzenberger...

More than ever before the atmosphere was electric as the field came on to the grid, with Senna occupying his 61st pole position, just ahead of Schumacher, Berger and Hill lined up behind them, and Lehto and the second Ferrari pilot Nicola Larini on the third row, the latter deputizing for Jean Alesi, who had injured his neck in a nasty shunt while testing at Mugello just before the Imola race.

Already, it had been a ghastly year for JJ, the pleasant Finn, for whom Benetton had finally seemed to offer the promise of the berth he had long deserved. The nightmare had begun in January with a testing accident at Silverstone that had severely damaged his neck. This was to be his return to action after the young Dutch driver Jos Verstappen had stood in for him in the first two races. JJ had done well to qualify fifth fastest, within a second of the man who that season would endorse his reputation for destroying his team-mates, but then had come Ratzenberger's death. Lehto, a sensitive, thoughtful and open fellow, had travelled to Imola with Roland and was distraught over his death, which had happened so soon after the loss of another friend, Evan Demoulaz, his former Formula Ford 2000 partner, who had died in June the previous year.

Just before the starting lights went green JJ's engine stalled, leaving him sitting exposed on the grid with both arms waving aloft. Of all the drivers such a thing could have happened to, he was the least deserving, and in the press room we thought of his neck injury and prayed desperately that nobody would hit him. By a miracle, it looked as though nobody would, though Heinz-Harald Frentzen avoided him by mere fractions of an inch in his Sauber, but then Pedro Lamy came bursting along in his Lotus, which he had qualified on the penultimate row. The Portuguese driver had been unsighted in all the rubber smoke and dust and ploughed straight into the Benetton's left rear wheel, pushing it up the track before his own car slithered to a halt minus its right-hand wheels. "Until that point I wasn't able to see that there was a stationary car on the grid at all," he said.

Neither of the drivers was injured; thankfully JJ's neck was not troubled and he sustained only a badly bruised right arm, but one of the wheels cleared the main grandstand and debris injured three spectators and a policeman. It also littered the pit straight. Lehto, however, already in an unhappy emotional state, would then witness the Senna accident on the television monitor.

The race should have been stopped while the track was cleaned, but instead it was continued behind an Opel safety car that barely had the speed to stay ahead of the pack being driven on half-throttle or less. And as the cars circulated at this slow pace, so tyre temperatures, pressures and therefore diameters dropped, which in turn meant that the so critical ride heights were disturbed. There are still some who believe that this could have been a factor in the tragedy that followed.

Senna had led Schumacher round that dramatic opening lap, followed by Berger, Hill, Frentzen, Hakkinen, Larini, Wendlinger, Katayama and Brundle, and as they went by the pits track workers toiled frantically to sweep away the mess.

For four more laps the pace car circulated ahead of the field, and as they went into their sixth lap Senna and Schumacher were finally allowed to resume racing again. Berger immediately dropped some way behind them, as did Hill, who admitted afterwards that he'd messed up the rolling restart.

Then the two leaders came round to begin their seventh lap, but as they went through *Tamburello* the Williams, instead of curving into the corner on the proper line, ran inexorably wider until it was off the road and almost instantly it smashed hard into the unyielding concrete wall that had always drawn such criticism. It was almost a replay of Berger's 1989 accident, but this time it happened further round the bend, closer to the exit, and the angle was more acute. As the Williams impacted it

23

exploded into a shower of debris before bouncing back into the path of oncoming vehicles.

In the press room we were concentrating on finishing listing the backmarkers in our lap charts when the cry came: "Senna!" And then we saw the replay of the impact and the aftermath.

This time they did stop the race, and the wait began as the television cameras homed mercilessly in on the unfolding drama. Somebody spoke encouragement as we saw that Senna's head had moved, and we all took that to mean that he was merely unconscious. But after a while his unmoving form, and the unhurried manner of the rescue workers, began to deliver a grim message; their lack of haste said it all. Later, of course, it would be suggested that a suspension component had penetrated Ayrton's helmet, inflicting fatal wounds, but at that time there was nothing but uncertainty, and an awful, shocked silence.

We are as disparate a bunch of fellow travellers as you are ever likely to find, those who make up the Formula One circus.

There are the mechanics, the men who love to express themselves through the talents of their hands, but whose work is rarely seen or appreciated by those on the outside, and all too often is denied the credit it merits from those on the inside, as well.

There are the team owners and managers, people who might have started out on the trail with the same intense passion for the sport that some of we hacks still nurture, but who either lost it along the way through sheer fatigue, battle weariness or the blight of tragedy, or perhaps because they became seduced and then corrupted by the influences of power and money, rather like high-class hookers or, in some cases, just cheap grifters. Like many of the 'public relations' hangers-on, they can be obtuse, shallow and, if it serves their purpose, downright dishonest. But by the same token they can, and do, say much the same of we writers, and in some cases they wouldn't necessarily be wrong, either.

Then there are the drivers, the men who can command the telephone-number salaries, but whose willingness and need to take risks ultimately entertains us all. These are the men who, in some cases, we supported and acted as psycho-analysts for at various stages of their careers, and with whom we shared phone conversations, confidences and gossip along the way. The sort of guys who, when they begin to make it, it suddenly dawns on you that when they move home you don't get the updated phone numbers.

Haves, have nots, and have a lots. A turbulent, egotistical, fanatical, self-opinionated bunch of individuals who are as likely to argue and kick against the traces as they are to pull together in anything approaching unison.

Until something like Imola happens. Then we are not the same people.

24

Emotions rise to the surface and, if only for a short time, we are united in our concern for a human life. Cynicism is stripped away and, sometimes, some horrible times, our grief is for a life taken, a life lost. For a precious while we forget the petty jealousies of competition, real or imagined. We put aside the masks we all wear, or else hold them closer still to our faces. As writers, instead of being unpaid publicists, or the subject of snubs because of the sometimes unpalatable accuracy and honesty of our stories, our words can be soothing, can trigger emotions, can strike chords. At times like this, we can put on paper the thoughts from a thousand heads.

And for a while we all stand together, one grieving, frightened, concerned family of itinerant motorsport travellers, until gradually time eases us back to our prejudices and our respective insular positions, and we move apart once more.

At such times there is a danger that death can become romanticized, but this is just a defence mechanism, and a means by which humanity seeks not to hurt the feelings of others or to offend sensibilities. There is nothing remotely romantic about death when it visits your circle. There is a poem I remember vaguely that goes along the lines: 'Death is not romantic. It is nothing, the endless time of never coming back. And when the wind blows through it you hear no sound.'

And when it is suddenly, brutally, horribly there in front of you, snatching one of the extended kin, you are forced to watch in close-up its effect on others.

Many of us, myself included, wrote of Ayrton Senna's desire to win, and suggested that if he had had to go, this was how he would have wanted it to be. But even as I wrote such things I kept hearing the words of the American writer Bob Brown, recording his feelings on the death of the great Bill Muncey, the Mario Andretti of Unlimited hydroplane racing: "People say Bill went the way he would have wanted to, out front, going for it," Bob wrote. "I don't buy that. I believe that, given a second chance, he would have squeezed the throttle that little bit less, would have leaned that little bit less on the boat. Would have gone around and bargained for more time."

And so, I guess, would Ayrton. Or Roland. Because that's the way real life is. We might take chances, especially drivers in the heat of battle, but nobody really throws caution that far to the wind yet wouldn't wish to retract a fatal step.

When the accident happens we stand around in quiet groups and that awful silence engulfs the track as the question begins to do the rounds. "Who is it?" And the wait begins.

Only in Senna's case it was deadly obvious who it was, for he had been the focus of the television camera at the very moment of impact. And this time the question was different. This time, even more so than it had been the previous day when we had been watching the monitors in the press room and had seen it all in replay, it was not even: "Which of two cars is it?" But: "How bad is it?"

And there, on the television screen, all emotion laid bare for an entire world to assimilate, was the cruel truth behind motorsport, the raw meaning behind the ticket warnings that say those simple but all too easily overlooked words: 'Motor racing is dangerous'. And the reminder that in such high-speed pursuits, the risk is sometimes total, no matter what some brilliant men try to do to make it otherwise.

They restarted the race at 2.55 and Michael Schumacher won it from Nicola Larini in the Ferrari and Mika Hakkinen in his McLaren. Karl Wendlinger and Ukyo Katayama were fourth and fifth, ahead of Damon Hill. The Briton, like Nigel Mansell with Ferrari back in 1989, had driven a gutsy race to set fastest lap after a clash with Hakkinen had delayed him, yet at no time could he be absolutely sure what had caused his team-mate's accident. Nor, by the same token, could he have had any way of knowing whether his own car might suffer the same fate. Without question, this was the performance of a brave man, though subsequently it would escape the notice of Renault Sport as it cast around for another star to replace Senna. Brave, too, was Brabham's drive.

The atmosphere had remained electric throughout the race, but only because everybody was so keyed-up waiting for yet another disaster. When it came, as Alboreto's Minardi lost a wheel in the pits on lap 49, it was scarcely believable, and many felt that the unwanted contest should have been abandoned there and then. But the 1994 San Marino Grand Prix ground on to the bitter end.

And as a sad postscript, that black weekend in Imola not only ended the careers of Roland Ratzenberger and Ayrton Senna, but ironically took the fight from JJ Lehto at the very place where he had scored his best ever F1 result three years earlier, and from Erik Comas, too. The Frenchman was shattered by the experience of seeing the post-accident trauma in close-up.

For some unfathomable reason, team owner Gerard Larrousse had despatched him from the pits following an early stop, and equally unfathomably, the marshal at the end of the pit road had allowed him out, even though the race had been red-flagged. He thus arrived going full-chat at the accident scene, and after the horror that he witnessed there he was never quite the same driver again.

Tim Holloway was an engineer with the team at that time and recalled: "Erik was hit up the rear in the original start, and all of the back of the car's floor was broken. So when the safety car was out initially we called him in because it seemed that the safety car would be out for some time. So we were all working on the car, and Gerard, in his usual French fashion, was really panicking. By this time the race was stopped and the other cars had formed up on a dummy grid on the straight before the last corner. We didn't know what was going on because we were so busy crawling under the car, but Gerard was looking at the monitors on the pit wall. Then he said: 'They're going to push the other cars to the grid, we've got to get out quick.' He was told that there was still plenty of time, because if they were going to push the cars we still had plenty of time to drive round and join them. 'No, no, we must get out. We can finish it on the grid.'

"So by this time none of the crew knew why the race had been stopped. Erik got to the end of the pit lane, and initially the marshal stood in front of him. But then he stepped back and waved him through. We shouldn't have sent him to the end of the pit lane, but the marshal shouldn't have let him out, either. Then Erik left the pits flat-out; he didn't know what was going on out there. While he was in the pits he had jumped out of the cockpit to start with, but then he jumped straight back in. It was completely not his fault, and then he saw Senna; after that Erik was in a terrible state.

"Gerard was the one to see it, and he was the one that wanted the car out... But they never should have let him out at the end of the pit lane. But let's be honest; on any restart nobody ever knows what's going on. You can never get an honest decision when a restart will be."

For Comas himself, a sensitive fellow, a member of the brotherhood of race drivers, and a man with a wife and a small son, that day was a devastating experience, for he, more than anyone, appreciated the true horror of the situation. Berger was the last driver to see Senna before the end, but Comas was the only one to see him at the accident scene. The other drivers knew there had been a big accident and that it involved Senna, but only Comas (and, to an extent, Lehto, by the television monitor) knew the real truth.

"I realized during the formation lap that a Ligier had touched me in the back, so when the start was done and I reached sixth gear, I felt a bad vibration at the back end of the car and decided to pit straight after the first lap. When the crash happened I was in the pit lane. All the emergency staff were at *Tamburello*, but all the mechanics were busy looking at my car, with just one idea: to make the car ready for when the racing started again. They didn't even look at the computers, or the pictures on television. None of us knew what had happened. I assume that the team managers, Larrousse and Tambay, knew there had been a crash, but not that the track was blocked by the emergency staff. So they let me go down the pit lane, and the worse thing is that the guy at the end of the pit lane let me go out. This is where they should not have allowed me to get out...

"I went out of the pits very quickly, again with just one idea: to get back on to the starting grid on time. I had no idea of what had happened, of how dramatic was the situation.

"First I nearly crashed into the ambulance car as I came round *Tamburello*, then I saw the helicopter and then I saw Ayrton on the grass. I stopped my car a few metres from his car, and he was close by. I was probably the last driver to see him, in the very few last moments...

"I was so shocked and... " – at this stage he broke off his narrative to make his choice of the English word very carefully – "ineffectual. Helpless. My spirit and body wanted to go to join him on the track, but there was nothing I could do, it was up to the doctors because he was already out of the car and down on the grass. I had stayed in my car for a very short time, until I realized what was happening, and then I completely cracked.

"Especially in this moment, I remember when I had my big crash in practice for the Belgian Grand Prix in 1992, when Ayrton came to stop my engine when I was unconscious. Just then, at Imola, the marshals took me to a road car, and when I got into it I saw on the seat beside me was Ayrton's helmet, and so when I realized how big was the crash for him, I just went away in this car, and I came back to the pit lane crying. Then I went to the motorhome and got away from the circuit as quickly as possible. I explained to Gerard that I was not in a condition to carry on racing. I said to him: 'I'm sorry, but I am not going to do this race. I can't do it.'"

As an interesting insight into the way a racing driver's psyche works, Comas found it very difficult to make the decision whether to continue in the sport, yet when he next drove a Formula One car in anger, in free practice at Monaco, he was initially sixth fastest. Like Berger, perhaps, an increase in adrenalin flow and aggression helped him through, where caution might have stymied him forever. "The first few days, though," he admitted, "it was terrible. I have to say that my wife, Brunella, has been marvellous, because in the situation I was not thinking what to do, but she knew what sacrifices I had made in all my life to do Formula One, and she explained me that only time would help the situation, and that I should not make a decision in this condition." Many other drivers expressed similar sentiments and drew heavily on their loved ones in the days after Imola, as the Senna tragedy reached out to touch them all.

"I wanted to be out of the car for some time longer than Monaco, but the team pushed me to test. I think it was on the Friday after the crash. And I think that was the best thing. But you need the help of your friends, your family and your wife. Monaco was okay, but the second, third, fourth and fifth of May were pretty difficult days."

Comas says he still thinks fondly of Ayrton Senna from time to time, as if the bond he felt will never be broken. "Of course I always thought about him, but once I am in a car I can close the door and concentrate on the job. But once you are able to do it again you have to keep everything out of your mind. I am doing that a lot of the time, but you cannot forget someone like that."

Comas agrees that, while Senna outwardly displayed a cold mien at times, beneath that carefully sculptured exterior lay a deeply compassionate man. "For sure, for sure. From the day that he maybe saved my life in Spa, after my crash, we always had many talks during the race weekends. I can remember at the morning debriefing by the race directors in Imola, he sat close to me and I suggested to him that it was a good time while we were all together to have a talk about the safety. And he answered me: 'I will call you this week and we will have a meeting in Monaco. Not here, but at the next race.' He was already decided to do something.

"I remember him well. When I crash at Spa he was not the first one on the scene. Many cars passed, including my own team-mate. but only Ayrton stopped."

That evening the press room and paddock were silent, yet full of shattered, stunned people moving like zombies as they tried to come to terms with the enormity of the situation. I had more than 10,000 words to write for *Motoring News* that weekend, and bar an obituary for Roland and my regular Saturday piece for *The Independent on Sunday* I hadn't written a thing. I had little taste for writing at that moment and had decided, since it was a Bank Holiday in England and *Motoring News* would be going to press a day later than usual, to crash into everything when I got home. Then a colleague prevailed upon me to write the obituary for Senna for *The Independent*. At the time it was the last thing I wanted to think about, yet in its way it proved cathartic. They wanted 1,200 words, by eight o'clock. I started at six and was finished by half-past. I can't remember ever writing anything else in my life where I was three or four coherent paragraphs ahead of myself all the way through. It was a start, and it helped. The adrenalin was flowing and the machine took over after that.

"I can remember clear as day standing on the startline waiting for the restart," Martin Brundle said. "At first I thought it was Hill's car there, not Senna's, because when I came through I was still busy dodging the wheels; there was a wheel on the track and some carbon-fibre still coming down out of the air. I was diving all over the place trying not to have yet another accident. And then I was standing on the startline and there was a serious lack of information."

Much would later be made of the smiles of Schumacher, Hakkinen and Larini on the podium, but few of the drivers at this stage really appreciated the seriousness of the situation, and many of them had deliberately been protected from the truth by their teams. It wasn't the sort of news you imparted on the radio link to a man who still had to go racing.

"I'd heard that he was all right because he'd moved his head," Brundle continued, "and that they were being very careful with him. And I have to say that I feel very sick even today to think that I raced 55 more times past a pool of Senna's blood. That doesn't please me at all.

"I was surprised by the number of British journalists who'd never seen a death in Formula One, who were coming up to me confused and looking for some kind of solace and comfort that just wasn't there. I'll never forget walking out of that place later that evening, and by then the rumours were around that he had actually died, but nobody could confirm it, and there were people, mostly girls and women, but all kinds of people, just standing and sitting and lying around just sobbing their eyes out."

Brundle spoke for most of the people round the world who had been so stunned and shaken by that terrible weekend when we spoke at Hockenheim in 1995. "I still don't actually quite believe it all, if the truth were known. Even here, 15 months later, I don't actually believe it. I still sometimes have to pinch myself to believe that actually happened, that whole day, or that whole weekend. I'd sort of had this association with Ayrton since my Formula Three days, and although I didn't realize it until afterwards my wife Liz had always had this enormous respect for him because she'd seen him all the way through, too. And I suddenly thought to myself: 'Christ, I've got a few Christmas cards from him, but I never even got his autograph.'"

Strangely enough, I did. I too had known him since the Formula Three days, and we'd had our ups and downs over the years, especially after the Warwick Affair in 1986, when he'd vetoed Derek joining Lotus, and then the two Suzuka Incidents in 1989 and 1990. At Suzuka in 1993, Honda published a book of its F1 exploits over the past decade and invited some journalists to a small gathering at which past and present Honda drivers were also to be present. Pretty soon everyone was getting their books signed and, partly out of mischief, I proffered mine to Ayrton and said with a smile: "You don't have to sign it if you don't want to."

He smiled back, relaxed, at that point carefree and yet to become embroiled again in controversy in his subsequent punch-up with Eddie Irvine. As he proceeded to scrawl with his left hand he said enigmatically, with the same smile: "Time is the big thing." How could we have known how little time was left to him.

DRAMA IN THE PIT LANE

Piling drama atop tragedy, Michele Alboreto's Minardi shed a wheel as the Italian attempted to speed back into the race following a routine refuelling and tyre change stop on the 49th lap. As he accelerated away, the right rear wheel of his car parted company with it and rolled and bounced a hazardous path down the crowded pit lane as the Minardi veered towards the Ferrari and Lotus pits with Michele frantically struggling to maintain control of it. The errant wheel then bounced high in the air and on to the track, but thankfully did not hit anybody else.

As an ambulance sped into the pit lane it looked like a scene from the tragedy at Indianapolis in 1973, when Armando Teran was struck and killed by a fire truck racing the wrong way to the site of Swede Savage's accident at Turn Four.

Here at Imola three Ferrari mechanics had been hurt: Maurizio Barbieri had a fractured left tibia and kneecap; Claudio Bisi had bruising to his left thigh and foot; and Daniele Volpi had suffered bruising internally and to the neck. In the Lotus pit, engineer Neil Baldry had fallen to the floor and hit his head; he was to be kept in hospital in Imola overnight, but was fit enough to fly home the following day.

Alboreto, a former Ferrari driver, of course, was beside himself afterwards, even though the incident was hardly his fault, and he called for speed limits in the pit lane. "I tried to save as many people as possible by turning the car away, and I am desperately sorry," he said.

Subsequently, speed limits in the pit road would become mandatory, and with good reason.

Warm-up

The town of Imola, on the Lombardy Plain close to the Appennine mountains, is divided (as indeed it has been since Roman times) by the Via Emilia autoroute, the great Roman road which begins its long journey many kilometres south to run up the Adriatic coast from Bari, through Pescara and Ancona, then Pesaro and on to the seaside resort of Rimini before turning inland for Imola, Bologna and, eventually, Milan. It is close to the part of the Emilia-Romagna region where the River Santerno wends its way down from the north, to flow gently by the race track that was conceived in 1948.

Despite this long-established geographic division, Imola has been united these many years by the inhabitants' love of motor racing, an emotion worn with the passionate yet unaffected and unselfconscious demonstrativeness that only Italians can carry off with any measure of panache.

The region is steeped in motorsport lore. In the great days of the Fifties the fabulous Mille Miglia race wound its tortuous way across Italy, its frequently changing route sometimes including a leg that took it through Ravenna, Forli, Pesaro, Ancona and Pescara, back up through from Florence to Bologna via the famed passes at Futa and Raticosa, then upward still to Padua.

Bari hosted Grand Prix races before the war, as did Pescara. Modena, the hallowed home to Ferrari, Maserati and Lamborghini, is only a short distance to the north-west between the two major towns Bologna and Milan, while Minardi's base is just to the south-east and Lamborghini's original home at Sant Agata is to the south-west. The Misano Adriatico track lies close to Rimini (and is a great deal closer to San Marino than is Imola!), and the Mugello track is between Bologna and Florence.

The town of Imola, which decks itself out with gay enthusiasm when the race comes to town, and was at a complete standstill for the first pukka Grand Prix in 1980, already had its own, rather gruesome, place in history long before the arrival of the race track won it an international flavour and reputation, for it was here that Cesare Borgia captured Imola Castle in 1500, and where its patron Saint Cassian was done to death.

Perhaps his lectures were terminally dull and needed livening up, or it may just have been the most supreme irony, but he was stabbed by students wielding their own pens. One is tempted to wonder whether they used his blood for ink afterwards.

Brutal, too, are the prices at the frighteningly expensive *San Domenico* restaurant in the centre of town, whose gastronomic reputation reaches the same broad horizons as the imagination of the man who penned its tariff. Most racers prefer to prolong their fiscal wellbeing by frequenting the charming *Ristorante Nardi* – the 'Ferrari restaurant' – on the Via Santerno, right outside the main gate. The food, in typical Italian fashion, is exquisite, and the local wine, *frizzante*, is a semi-sparkling drink not to be confused with the full sparkling *spumante*.

The San Marino link is, by the most charitable interpretation, a mite tenuous, and it was typical of Enzo Ferrari's fertile imagination which quickly came up with a good reason – and who would ever dare to argue with it or its logic and desirability, let alone want to? – why Italy should have two Grands Prix. The Principality – the smallest republic in the world – is only 15 miles inland of the seaside resort of Rimini, but more like 50 miles from Imola itself. Yet with that wonderful *laissez faire* attitude of the Italians, who really minds? Twice in its history the Pope's forces have invaded, yet San Marino has maintained its fiercely protected independence, and it is fitting that Monte Carlo is the only other Principality in the world to enjoy the cachet of holding its own Grand Prix.

Both Imola and Monza are home to a rare breed of superfan, collectively known as the *tifosi*. All race tracks across the globe have their enthusiasts, the people who save up and pay to see the racers in action because racing excites them. In Britain the real *cognoscenti* know as much about the racing as many people within the paddock; in France you get the feeling that most spectators are there just because it makes a nice day out. In Hungary you get the impression from the banners opposite the pits that the spectators know a great deal about the politics of the sport, just as in Spain (especially Jerez) you are sometimes tempted to believe that it wouldn't take long to get on personal terms with the entire crowd. In Britain and Germany, too, you also get the rough, xenophobic element, the sort who like to invade tracks, throw beer cans and string up banners with that four-letter word beginning with F that isn't Ford uppermost in the message, and who are there just to see one of their own giving Johnny Foreigner a hard time.

And in Italy you get the *tifosi*, possibly the best informed fan of all who, though he or she likes a good time, never seems to lose their laidback attitude (unless the Ferraris are out), and who always seems to find a way to see the action. Those who do not camp out on the hills within the Imola circuit get by with special little wooden seats that look as if they are swings stolen from the local park, except that the chains have hooks on the ends so that they can be slung over the top of Imola's concrete walls to provide an excellent view until the occupants get moved on, in which case it's just a matter of relocating somewhere else along the wall. The *tifosi* love all things Ferrari and support the Prancing Horse team and its drivers wholeheartedly, until they break down, and then beware of their vocal wrath. They don't care about Italian drivers unless they are in Ferraris, or unless the Ferraris have retired and there's nothing else left to cheer. Ask Riccardo Patrese about 1983, and he'll tell you what it's like to be on the receiving end...

But generally the *tifosi* is a warm-hearted breed that loves motor racing, and it makes you feel good just to be among them. A difference between the *tifosi* at Imola and Monza? The Imola *tifosi* tend to be more friendly and you don't walk around clutching your belongings quite so hard. Even the criminal element seem less intent on stealing your car, although if they do, you can be sure that they'll do it in style, like in 1995, when both Gerhard Berger and Jean Alesi were each relieved of their Ferraris – no favouritism there!

In 1994, where our story started, the track at the *Autodromo Dino e Enzo Ferrari* measured 3.132 miles as it plunged and climbed its way along by the River Santerno and then up and over the crest that created such a natural spectator arena in the first place. The circuit is unusual for a European road course insofar as it runs anti-clockwise and has its pits and paddock located on the outer perimeter. Of all the other World Championship venues, only Interlagos, in Brazil, also runs the 'wrong' way round.

Past the pits, the road led to the notorious *Tamburello* curve, a flat-out yet nevertheless undemanding left-hander that seemed to go on forever before spitting cars down the straight towards the curving right-hander that was named in honour of the late Gilles Villeneuve, following the ferocious accident that he survived there during Imola's first official Grand Prix in 1980. Then came the heavy braking for *Tosa*, the left-hand hairpin that led uphill and through a gentle right arc towards the left-hander at *Piratella*, and then the sweeping plunge down towards the little chicane at *Acque Minerali*, the Mineral Water corner which always sounds such a lot more glamorous in the Italian tongue. From there it was another climb, this time to the second chicane, the *Variante Alta*, which preceded another swooping downhill rush to the *Rivazza*, which was in fact two 90-degree left-hand corners, which all but completed the lap. On exiting the second *Rivazza*, drivers then accelerated towards a gentle right-hander and another, longer, chicane called *Bassa*, before the 90-degree left-right flicks called *Traguardo*, which returned them to the start/finish line by the pits.

It was never difficult to appreciate just what a steely little circuit Imola must have been in its pre-chicane heyday, when Helmut Marko set the lap record at 127mph with the CanAm BRM in 1972 and the run from *Acque Minerali* to *Rivazza* was just a flat-out climb followed by a flat-out dive, but even in 1994, with the *Minerali*, *Alta* and *Bassa* chicanes, Imola was still quick, a demanding circuit where horsepower, braking power and chassis balance were of equal importance. Ayrton Senna set pole position for that 1994 event, achieving 138mph despite all the artificial restraints. It was not a place for the faint of heart but, rather, a place where those with spirit and a zest for living would find their presence made welcome, and their courage and commitment well rewarded.

2
Il Drake and The Dreamers

"Fantastic! This place can become a true little Nurburgring."
– Enzo Ferrari

All good things begin with a dream, and in the story of Imola there were four dreamers who shared their ideas one summer evening in 1948 when the air was balmy and the rush of peace had begun once again to turn young men's fancies from war to motorsport. What Alfredo Campagnoli, Graziano Golinelli, Ugo Montevecchi and Gualtiero Vighi saw that night, as they strolled through the *Parc Acque Minerali* in Imola, chattering about motorcycle racing, was the creation of a new track where their beloved bikes could be raced without the restrictions that hampered efforts at competition elsewhere in the town. And as their dream became more widely known, it was supported by the vision, determination, organizational skills and purse of Dr Francesco Costa, an indefatigable motorcycle enthusiast known universally to his allies as 'Checco'. His son Claudio is now the motorcycle equivalent of Prof Watkins, and in the 1975 200 Mile race he saved the life of Vinicio Salmi after a bone-breaking fall at *Piratella*.

With Tommaso Maffei Alberti as president, the Imola Sport and Tourist Association (ESTI) was created, and Costa and other members of the Motor Club of Imola also made considerable input. Indeed, Costa was so determined to have his own track that he almost ruined himself. They formed a plan and put it before CONI, the Italian national Olympic Committee, and the local council, where it was received enthusiastically by mayor Amedeo Tabanelli. The CONI didn't put up a huge amount of money – that came mainly from the community (ESTI) and, later, from Shell – but the CONI's support would prove vital.

Later in 1948, Giulio Onesti, president of the CONI, announced a grandiose scheme to build not one, but 12 race tracks in Italy; Imola would be the prototype. "There was talking, talking. Lots of politics. Was a big political move by Onesti and the CONI," recalled veteran Italian journalist Franco Lini. "There was opposition. But finally, at the end of 1949, they began to do things."

There were numerous obstacles, among them arguments with land owners; some were genuinely reluctant to sell, while others clearly saw an opportunity to up their ante while holding out for greater remuneration. One party even approached the State Tribunal to try to reverse Onesti's largesse, but he was a wily politician who knew how to protect himself, and nothing came of it. Typical of the smaller difficulties at that stage was the church which lay within the grounds of the track and presented problems for racegoers and churchgoers alike. At one point the latter received special passes to enable them to attend services of a non-automotive type. Lini suggested: "Most of the people don't go to church until then!" One shudders to think what the FIA would make of that today! Eventually the problem was solved by an agreement in 1959 to create a new parish centre on the Piazza Michelangelo in town.

It would be 1950 before the first sod was broken to initiate construction, and fittingly the tool was wielded by Onesti. It has often been suggested that this most important dignitary had become involved in the project following a direct approach from Enzo Ferrari, *Il Drake*. Whether this was true or simply more of the puff associated with Ferrari's mystique is impossible to determine from this distance, but certainly Ferrari was always in the background, prepared to offer assistance and support in persuading people to help the venture. "But Ferrari never put his hand in his own pocket!" said Lini, who in 1966 and 1967 was team manager for the Scuderia.

In 1952 both Ferrari and Onesti were present again when famous personalities in the form of newly crowned World Champion Alberto Ascari, his mentor Luigi Villoresi and the very first World Champion, Dr Giuseppe Farina, tested the track for the first time that October in Ferrari 340 Sports under the watchful eyes of the late Count Gianni Lurani. There had been motocross events since 1949, but on April 25, 1953 the Motor Club of Imola held its first proper race, and befitting the vision of its founders, it was for motorcycles. The track was an amalgam of some existing roads by the River Santerno and some in the *Castellaccio* park, hence its initial name of *Castellaccis*. It measured 3.12 miles (surprisingly close to its 1994 measurement of 3.132 miles, despite all the changes in the intervening years) and was officially opened by Tabanelli's successor, Veraldo Vespignani. A year later, Costa hit on the idea of a well-funded competition in conjunction with the Shell oil company, and the lucrative Golden Shell series was born.

Even though Enzo Ferrari continued to be a tireless presence in the background of Imola's history, since Maranello was so close, the numerous political arguments within the community continued to delay the full development of the track during its early years, and they would rage on and off until a referendum was held in the town in 1972. In 1970, however, would come a particularly shrewd piece of public relations when ESTI decided to rename the circuit in honour of Ferrari's son Dino, who had succumbed to leukaemia in 1956. In a ceremony of investiture, mayor Amedeo Ruggi presided over the christening of the *Castellaccis* circuit as the *Autodromo Dino Ferrari*. Franco Gozzi, Ferrari's right-hand man, recalled: "It was a private affair of Mr Ferrari, but I was involved with the second part when Mr Ferrari met people from Imola. If I remember well it was Giulio Onesti, the Minister of Sport at the time; he was the big boss of money and sport in Italy. Mr Ferrari was able to persuade Onesti to release some money to start Imola, and this was absolutely the origin of the track. There is a long story about the different mayors of Imola, who changed every four or five years. These people were encouraged by Ferrari to go ahead with the project at Imola. There is a very early photograph of Mr Ferrari, Giulio Onesti and Luciano Conti, who would later run the circuit for the holding company, Sagis, walking on the open road there one year, the first time that Mr Ferrari was invited to see the place. And the answer of Ferrari was: 'Fantastic! This can become a true little Nurburgring.'"

Though Imola in those far-off early days had a reputation more as a motorcycle track than as a car racing venue, its history embraced four wheels as early as 1954 when the Automobile Club of Bologna held the first of its Golden Shell races for sportscars on June 20.

Ferrari, Maserati and Osca all brought cars, to be driven by names guaranteed to satisfy a crowd whose intense enthusiasm for racing was already making itself apparent. Luigi Musso, Eugenio Castellotti, Cesare Perdisa and Umberto Maglioli graced the field, while Colin Chapman was also a contestant in one of the races, as was a newcomer from Australia, Jack Brabham, giving the meeting a truly international flavour. Maglioli dominated the first race in his Ferrari, with Musso's Maserati some way behind, but Perdisa took the second for the Trident. Osca's turn for glory came in the third event, which Castellotti won from the emergent newcomer Brabham, Musso and Giulio Cabianca. Colin Chapman's long journey to Imola proved less successful, but he left for home considerably impressed by the challenge the circuit presented.

Motorcycles, however, were the staple diet at that stage, and one of the characters who breathed life into Imola, ultimately at the expense of his own, was Ray Amm.

"A hell of a lot of those we used to think of as colonials came over to ride in the TT, before and after the war, and Ray Amm was one of them," recounted Murray Walker, whose late father Graham was as renowned for his motorcycle racing commentaries as Murray is today for his Grand Prix work. Walker Jnr also has no mean knowledge of motorcycle matters.

"Amm just appeared from Southern Rhodesia; we knew nothing about him. He rode 350 and 500 Nortons, and immediately established himself as a bloody good, if unbelievably wild, rider. You were always amazed when you saw him come round again the next lap.

"I remember him for his lantern jaw, a white crash helmet which had some sort of chequer pattern round the rim of it and, I think, the coat of arms of Rhodesia. He had an extremely nice wife, whose name was Jill, unless I'm very much mistaken, and he was tough. He had to be, because if you were a privateer in those days the way you made your money was to go on the Continent and race in all sorts of obscure events in France, primarily, as well as Belgium and Holland. Some in Germany, too, I think. And Ray did that extremely well. He caught the eye of Joe Craig, who was the fabled Norton tuner. Something happened to make Ray get the works ride; I think it was that Geoff Duke left and went to Gilera, and they needed someone and took Ray because he was obviously bloody quick.

"I remember him being about the only person in the world who'd got the guts to ride the infamous 'kneeler' Norton because it handled like a five-bar gate, and streamlining in those days was a black art. And it had this bloody great proboscis sticking out in front..."

Amm, therefore, fell into the category of the abnormally brave, and was a racer who never quite knew where the limit lay. After his arrival in Europe in 1951 he had matched team-mate Duke's pace the following year, winning the 350cc class in the Italian GP at Monza. In 1953 he achieved a rare double by winning the Junior 350 and Senior 500 races at the TT, and though he later broke a collarbone after setting a trail of lap records across Europe, he promptly set 1,000km records in the 350cc (124mph) and 500cc (133mph) classes for Norton on the bumpy French Montlhery track as his means of getting back to work. In 1954 he won all his four races at Interlagos, in Sao Paulo, two in the 350cc and two in the 500cc classes, before finishing second to Umberto Massetti's Gilera at Imola. Shortly after that he had overwhelmed even Duke in foul weather conditions to win a controversial Senior TT.

This, then, was the nature of the man who faced the field in the 350cc race at Imola on April 11, 1955, the man who was destined to be the first to die there. Amm liked to lean his bikes over so far that the footrests scraped the track, and though he'd come to grief doing that riding a 350 Norton in the German GP at Solitude the previous year, he was doing it again at Imola as he chased after Australian rider Ken Kavanagh, who had come to Europe at the same time that he had. After Norton's withdrawal at the end of 1954, Amm had been snapped up by MV Agusta, and he was desperate to show well on Italian soil. At the *Rivazza* he scraped the footrest once too often, slid off the wet track, and hit a metal post. It struck him a blow just below the protective rim of his 'pudding basin' helmet, and he was dead by the time he reached hospital.

"It was his first MV event at the track and he was extremely unfortunate," John Surtees remembered. "He just happened to hit a post in the wrong place. Ray was a real racer, but a very competent one, and again there was a series of circumstances. Perhaps he still wasn't that well acquainted with the bikes, and it was a change, as I found, coming from the Nortons. One just can't tell. He was on the 350 at the time, which needed rowing along pretty hard to make it competitive. It needed riding extremely hard to keep up with some of the faster machines."

Walker had another tale which added colour to Amm's memory. "I remember him one time coming back in his transporter, if you can call it that; it was a sort of three-ton truck. And when he landed at Harwich, or wherever it was, Customs said: 'Would you step this way, sir, we'd like to have a look at your van.' And they'd obviously been tipped off because they found a secret compartment full of watches. I mean, people didn't bring in drugs in those days; you were considered very wicked if you brought in watches. I'm afraid the passage of time has eroded what happened to him, but I'm pretty sure he didn't go inside. I think that was about the time he went to Agusta."

In those days motorcycles generally handled badly, and apart from his abnormal bravery, that was one of the reasons for Amm's demise. Agusta then produced a copy of the original Gilera four, which Nello Paggani and Massetti rode with great speed but little distinction. "The thing went bloody quickly on the straight and incredibly slowly around the corners," Walker recalls, "partly because the bike didn't handle particularly well, and partly because the Italians hadn't got the guts to ride it quickly around them. Then Agusta copied it and Carlo Bandirola rode it – he'd got more courage than the rest of them put together – but the bike handled even worse than theirs did, so he never got very far."

In desperation, the Italians turned to British engineering and put Les Graham, the father of former Chevrolet Camaro racer Stuart, aboard it. Prior to his death at Bray Hill during the TT he developed the bike with leading-link front forks designed by Brummie Ernie Earls, which made it handle much better. But it was not until Surtees brought all of his considerable talents to bear at MV that the Italians really got things right, and in the ensuing years Big John 'owned' Imola on the occasions when he was permitted to ride there.

In 1958 he was still the fastest thing on two wheels after taking the 500cc World Championship in 1956. On April 25 he and MV Agusta teammate Remo Venturi romped home first and second ahead of Jack Ahearn's Norton, a result they were to repeat two years later after John Hartle's challenge to the Italian ended when he fell off his Norton. In between, however, Imola had seen tragedy in the 1959 race. Surtees won for MV, as usual, with Hartle second for Norton and the promising Gary Hocking third, also on one of the British bikes. But during a spirited fight for third, Harry Hinton Jnr had crashed at *Rivazza*, the spot where

Amm had perished four years earlier. Surtees was so alarmed by the incident that he stopped at the pits to report it at the end of the lap, before continuing to victory.

"They didn't hold championship races there, just non-championship, and some of the teams would support them," he remembered. "Some of the time I was allowed to go there, and some of the time I wasn't. It was still in its original form as it started, without any chicanes. You'd come up over the top of the hill and then just drop down and sweep through the *Rivazza*, which was really one curve. Then it was one big, long curve all the way back past the pits to *Tamburello* and *Tosa*, then the climb and drop back to *Acque Minerali*. It was quick! It was extremely quick! And it was bumpy. A very, very testing circuit. All circuits which are quick are obviously the challenging ones, and to actually get those corners right, particularly over the top of the hill and then down the hill, were the all-important things. That's where you made up all the time, because they were quick. And if you made a mistake... Well, there wasn't much run-off.

"You've always got a problem with those types of circuit, where they can be pretty dirty and dusty, and it takes a while for them to get clean. *Tamburello* didn't present a massive problem, though, because even then the circuit was a reasonable width. You could really lean into it, and the line wouldn't be any different to in a car, except that with a car you've got two wheels outside you and with a bike you've got purely two wheels and are using every bit of the road, so you can straight-line a corner much more effectively with a bike than you can with a car. But then, of course, you had a problem stopping at the end for *Tosa*, particularly in those days, when you used full streamlining! There, of course, it was relatively hard on brakes, and with full streamlining the bike would really be travelling on down there. On those type of bikes you'd be talking in the 160s... And the problem was that you had all sorts of cambers, and originally the corner was tighter than it is today, when they've opened up the inside and given a bit more chamfer. It was always a good overtaking place, that, and over the hill after it, and in those days all those corners were more pronounced."

Another man who raced a motorcycle there back in 1956 was Bernard Charles Ecclestone, even then a busy entrepreneur who was finding his way by simultaneously dabbling in car racing with his own Cooper 500 as well as owning the Connaught Grand Prix team and managing the career of Stuart Lewis-Evans. Though he now recalls few of the details of racing his Manx Norton, the crowds still stick in his mind.

"It was a bit naughty! I remember the people climbing over the fence, all that business. That was the ticket control! And the crowds afterwards... We parked outside; in those days we didn't have a paddock or anything. But in those days everywhere was like that, that was nothing special. It was just a little bit chaotic. It was like all the circuits; when people got to the grid, that's when the race started. Whether it was two or three o'clock, it didn't matter... television [of motorsport] wasn't invented then."

At the beginning of 1960 a press conference was held in Milan by the CONI. Franco Lini was there, working for the magazine *AutoItaliana*. "People like me were thinking of the promise of the CONI to do the 12 tracks. They never finish the first one properly! There was Onesti, talking about the Olympic facility in Rome. At the end of the story, I said: 'Mr Onesti, you promised to build 12 racing tracks. Do you call Imola the prototype? At least you want to finish it properly.'

"Like every political man, at the end he say: 'Oh, Mr Lini, of course! As soon as we finish with the Olympic, we do it!' They never did!"

Nevertheless, the curtain had been raised, and nine years after Ferrari, Maserati and Osca had fought out that first big sportscar race, an international field of racing drivers formed a grid at Imola, on April 21, 1963, for the first Formula One race, the non-championship *IV Gran Premio d'Imola*.

There was great disappointment in store for the *tifosi* when Ferrari withdrew its 156s that had been slated for Surtees and Willy Mairesse, ostensibly because they weren't ready, but possibly because *Il Drake* did not wish to risk a drubbing in his own backyard. Without the red cars the entry was very similar to the previous week's Pau GP, and was headed by the works Lotus 25-Climaxes of Jimmy Clark and Trevor Taylor, but also there were Jo Bonnier, in Rob Walker's Cooper T60, and Jo Siffert, in his Ecurie Filipinetti Lotus 24, teamed with Carel de Beaufort's Porsche 718. Jack Fairman drove a similar car after testing the ATS, which was still not ready and wouldn't appear publicly until Spa in June. Other notables were private entrant Bob Anderson with his Lola and the emergent Lorenzo Bandini in Guglielmo Dei's old Cooper T53, partnered by Carlo Abate in an even older T51.

Clark was in his usual blistering form in qualifying, when his lap of 1m 48.3s was 2.5 seconds faster than Taylor's quickest. Bonnier, who shared the front row with them, was a further second behind the Yorkshireman, with Siffert and Bandini on the second row, two and three seconds respectively adrift of the Swede; it was not a close-matched grid.

Nor was it a close race, for Jimmy simply lit off into the distance, as he was to do so many times during his meteoric career. The quick nature of the track was very much to the Scot's liking and he led each of the 50 laps to score another of his dramatically easy victories at an average of 99mph.

Taylor might well have repeated his excellent drive at Pau, where he had finished only a tenth of a second behind his team leader, although the result on that occasion had been slightly stage-managed, such had been the superiority of the two Lotuses. This time, however, Trevor had yet another recurrence of the team's infamous Colotti 'queerbox' problems, and he ended up losing some of his gears. Yet despite this handicap he set the fastest lap, equalling Jimmy's pole position time, and thus going 2.5 seconds quicker than he himself had managed during practice. There were to be shades in his drive that day of Michael Schumacher's performance whilst stuck in fifth gear during the Spanish Grand Prix in 1994.

"We only went there once, and the funny thing is that when you see it on television you can't figure out which way it goes," said Taylor in later years. "You see a corner and think: 'Didn't we used to go straight on there?' It was the same when I went to Nurburgring last year; I got there, and for the first three or four miles round the circuit I was completely lost. Then all of a sudden it all started to come back to me, and then I could have taken you round the circuit blindfolded.

"That fastest lap at Imola, I got it with only three gears! I was well up to start with, and then the gearbox began playing up again and I started to drop back. I remember that Rob Walker said: 'It's bloody marvellous, isn't it! He got fastest lap on three gears, and we've all got six!'

"It was a good lap, that. It was one of those strange things, believe you me. You know, you're using your gearbox sometimes as a brake, to save your brakes themselves, and I think it was one of those occasions when you went into the corners a little bit quicker, but you weren't wheelspinning coming out, you were putting rubber on the ground... One of those things. I remember, we were sitting having a meal in the night-time afterwards, and Rob said again: 'This is unbelievable. Why do we have six-speed gears when you can do that on three?'

Andrea de Adamich, whose career encompassed successful spells with Alfa Romeo in sportscars, Formula One with Ferrari in 1968, and F1 and F5000 with Surtees, before he switched to journalism, raced saloon cars at that 1963 race prior to his graduation to F3. "What happened with Trevor meant that the circuit was giving to the drivers the opportunities..." he said. "Monza was the big name but, technically, Imola was more."

Subsequently, the transmission problem dropped Taylor back to a lowly ninth place, 14 laps behind Clark, and it was left to Siffert to bring his Lotus-BRM home second, 1m 26s adrift. Anderson was a lap behind, keeping his Lola-Climax ahead of Jo Schlesser and Carlo Abate, and Carel De Beaufort was sixth. Bonnier had held on to second place until the engine in Walker's Cooper broke a piston on the 21st lap, while Bandini's hopes of glory in front of his countrymen were dashed by falling oil pressure after only eight laps.

In the years that followed, Imola's motorcycle races would continue to draw huge crowds as it hosted World Championship rounds, while a meeting between Costa and the American race promoter Bill France in

1970 led to 'Daytona coming to Europe' as Imola initiated its 200 Mile race in 1972. Some of the sport's greatest names – Giacomo Agostini, Kenny Roberts, Johnny Cecotto, Marco Lucchinelli, Steve Baker, Graeme Crosby, Phil Read, Eddie Lawson and the superfast but fated Jarno Saarinen (who was killed at Monza in 1973) – raced and won there. And its domestic car events, for single-seaters and saloon cars, helped many an aspiring Grand Prix star to cut his teeth.

De Adamich retains fond memories of the Imola of that period; it was a time when motor racing thought little of the safety aspects, and when the characters of tracks differed far more than they do in today's television-homogenized era.

"It was very quick and very different from Monza; it was quick but twisty. Remember that Monza in my period had no chicanes. I race in Monza flat-out from the *Parabolica* until the first of *Lesmos*, and flat-out from the second of *Lesmos* until the *Parabolica*, because *Ascari* was a flat-out corner. Imola, at that time, was a quick circuit compared to today's layout, but in respect to Monza and Spa, was a medium circuit with a lot of corners.

"It was really challenging, because a driver was really thinking to drive. *Tamburello*, with these kind of cars, was not a flat-out corner, and nor were all the others, the *Minerali*, etc. It was a difficult and dangerous circuit because you had the time to think during corners and to watch what you had outside of you. We are talking from the period from 1963 up to 1973-74, from saloons to the 1,000kms sportscars such as the 3-litre Alfa Romeo T33 I raced against Jacky Ickx.

"At the same time, to have an up and down situation was really giving to the driver something that only the Nurburgring was giving. The aim for the mini Nurburgring was achieved; you had no slow corners apart from the *Tosa* after the straightline, and in any case was never a real hairpin. For us it was the small Nurburgring, because we could have the same fun to drive there, but with human dimension, six kilometres or whatever.

"The run-off areas were limited, yes, and we could write a book just on that concept! Sometimes, going back to that period, it is impossible to the mentality of today to accept to race in that condition. In Italy, the two main circuits were Monza and Imola. Enna-Pergusa was too far away; it was something limited in the season.

"There were trees, no guardrails. In some areas, if you were going out of the road, you would crash into the trees. *Acque Minerali*, for example, had a low stone wall on its outer edge, although there was debris fencing, which was quite advanced for its time.

"Also the angles was not correct. It was not only the type of barrier, but the philosophy of the safety mentality, which was that if you had no space for run-off then the closer the barrier would be to the circuit, the less angle of impact there would be between car and barrier. That would be safer for the driver. But in that case the small mistake would be paid for. Okay, you had barriers there, but sometimes on the straight, out of the fast corner, you had nothing. *Tamburello*, in my period, had only a small guardrail; you could finish in the Santerno river!

"But you had to consider this, too: that on motorways in the same period you were facing the problem of danger between the two lines of traffic. Everything was in proportion. The airplanes going overseas were not the same of today. Everything in the safety mentality was of the same proportion. In my period there were not so many motorways; in my day the motorway finished in Bologna and you had to go by small road all the way to Imola. It was some journey, 30 years ago!

"My favourite corner was the part going before the straight, the *Rivazza*. From the *Minerali* you were going flat-out, no chicanes, and then down to the *Rivazza*. And after that you were crossing the straightline in front of the pits where it was possible to have a tow down to *Tosa*; those were the best corners. *Tosa* was the big braking, but always dangerous, because the curve now called *Villeneuve* was flat-out, but with the cars we had then the grip and aerodynamics were not the same as today. The cars' tendency was to go out of line, cutting the braking for *Tosa*. It was a little bit dangerous to try and overtake there because the risk was that the driver in front of you couldn't keep his car to the right part of the corner and you could risk a collision. You couldn't win a race at Imola because of the tow, like you could at Monza, and you couldn't race without wings, once they had come, like you could at Monza."

Such are the stories of any race track, for they are natural arenas where man competes and where such anecdotes are forged. But the people who paid to watch helped to make Imola special, too, as de Adamich summarizes.

"The nice aspect of Imola, in respect to other circuits, was also the public. And that remains still today. There is a difference of culture. In that period there was not such movement of public coming from abroad. Was very much local public and Emilio Romagna – Ferrari house – [the circuit] was still not yet named after Dino Ferrari, was just Santerno circuit, Imola circuit. But the racing culture of the public there was higher than in other areas. Higher than Monza. In Monza you had much more public coming from Switzerland, from Austria, from Germany, generally speaking. But in Imola it was like, for a singer, going in a small theatre like Parma, Regimiglia, and not so big like *La Scala*, but the public is much more critical. And normally, a new opera is going there to find out if it is going to be successful, like Broadway, say it like that. Well, Imola was a little bit like that for us as Italian drivers, giving us the same feeling. If you were going well in Imola, for sure you were accepted as a good driver from the Italian public."

That, then, was Imola in its early days. A challenging track, that did realize the dreams of Alfredo Campagnoli, Graziano Golinelli, Ugo Montevecchi and Gualtiero Vighi, that responded to the skills of Checco Costa, and which lived up to Enzo Ferrari's hopes to create a mini Nurburgring, even if it didn't spawn replicas elsewhere according to Onesti's grandiose plans.

ANDREA'S SLICK MOVE

Tyre technology had a long way to go back in the mid-Sixties, and the rubber of the day and the type of tyres in use were more durable and less susceptible to variations in surface conditions as compounding, construction and tread design were still in their infancy. One of Andrea de Adamich's favourite memories concerns his foresighted attempt to try 'slicks' in a Formula Three event.

"Okay, we did not have the feeling, like today, of the dirty track, with only one racing line and dirt either side of it. I was racing there before slick tyres, which came through from Firestone from Indy, moving to Formula One. Even then the slick tyres looked like a small flower; you still had a small cutting on the tread.

"I remember something nice happening for me in Imola with Formula Three. I had a nice set of Firestone tyres for my Formula Three Brabham that I had taken to Zolder and then used there in a saloon race. There was also a Formula Two and Formula Three race there and I was racing, and winning, with the Alfa Romeo GTA. Then I took the tyres with me for my Formula Three race in Imola. The technical *commissaires* were not giving me the permission to drive on the tyres because for them, with no knowledge, they appeared to be worn out because they had no tread left. The regulation then was that you needed a minimum of tread – one or two millimetres – to be accepted to race. And I had a big fight on that, which I won. They let me race them after I had explained that they were a new tyre for dry conditions. I admitted that I would have a big problem if it rained, but I convinced them that was my problem. There was no regulation then about dry and wet races..." He won.

3
Heats, Hopes and Hotel Hutch

"I don't remember anything until in the evening. People tell me I walked myself down to the pits. I don't know." – Henri Pescarolo

Six years after that non-championship F1 event, serious international racing returned when Imola hosted a 500km endurance event for sportscars, which was won by the Gulf Mirage of Jacky Ickx from the close-following Alfa Romeo T33/3 of Ignazio Giunti. A year later the circuit staged the seventh and penultimate round of the 1970 European Formula Two Championship. Whereas the *IV Gran Premio d'Imola* had been run over 50 laps, this race was to establish a pattern to which the circuit owners would hold dear for several years, with an aggregate result being taken from two 30-lap heats. These were won by Clay Regazzoni and Emerson Fittipaldi, in Tecno and Lotus respectively, with the overall victory going to Regga from Emmo. Derek Bell's third place in his Church Farm Racing Brabham BT30 helped to keep his slim championship hopes alive before they headed to Hockenheim, where Clay would duly take the title. Ronnie Peterson struggled home fourth in the unloved March 702, ahead of the Brabhams of Rolf Stommelen and the American Tasman racer Mike Goth. The fastest lap fell to Jacky Ickx in his BMW, in 1m 35.5s.

The following year an incident occurred which left an indelible impression on Jeff Hutchinson, now a veteran of F1 reporting, but then just beginning to hit his stride as a freelance photo-journalist. This was on September 12, when the Austrian Klaus Reisch, heir to the Spar grocery chain, died whilst driving his Alfa T33 during Imola's Interserie sportscar race.

"It was a grey, miserable, raining day, and I was probably the only person standing at the pit wall. I'd gone there to take a picture of him, and for some reason he had spun earlier that lap. He'd got out and not put his seatbelts back on, a bit like Graham Hill at Watkins Glen. There were big standing puddles all over the straight, and as he came out of the long corner before the pits he spun and aquaplaned straight towards me. He hit the wall right at my feet, and all I did was duck down behind it. I was the only one there because it was pouring with rain, and all these bits of bodywork came flying over the top of my head and landed behind me with other bits of debris.

"After that impact I stood up again and the car was then continuing to spin down the road. It hit the barrier just at the base of what is now the Marlboro Tower, but used to be race headquarters, just after the end of the pit wall. The flames went up, oh, it must have been almost to the height of the tower itself. The car caught fire immediately, and it was an enormous ball of flame, but unfortunately, because he hadn't been wearing seatbelts, Klaus had been flung out. As the car hit the pit wall it had spun round in one of these high-speed spin jobs, and he got thrown backwards out of the car and clouted the back of his head on the rollbar. He was left lying face-down just off to the left side of the track, in front of the main grandstands.

"Everyone went rushing down to the flaming car, thinking he was inside, and for three or four minutes utter confusion reigned as they were trying to put the fire out. Meanwhile, everybody in the grandstand was doing their famous Italian catcalls, trying to draw the organizers' attention to the fact that the driver was lying in the middle of the track.

"At that time, the ambulance crew, who had rushed to the burning car, then realized that Klaus was in the middle of the track, right opposite where I was standing, did a U-turn on the circuit, almost collected Arturo Merzario in the 2-litre Abarth (who very nearly had a big accident and almost ran over Klaus Reisch at the same time), and then eventually they red-flagged the race and carted him off.

"I think Klaus was killed instantly, and I remember they cleared all the debris. It had stopped raining, and they had put cement dust down where Klaus had been. I remember that it was all sort of pink, where blood had come through the cement dust, and they pushed Jo Bonnier's car out on to the grid to start the second part of the race. They pushed him across this pink dust and he just turned to Heini Mader and said: 'I don't want to do this,' and they just pushed the car away and he didn't race." Poignantly, less than a year later the safety-conscious Bonnier was himself killed when his Lola collided with a Ferrari during the 1972 Le Mans race.

As would be the case with Roland Ratzenberger, it was said that Reisch died in the ambulance on the way to the hospital, but those who saw his accident believed that he had succumbed instantly. For many years legal complications dogged Luciano Conti as a result of the chaos that ensued in the immediate aftermath.

Hutchinson recalled the contrast of Imola then and today. "In those days the only press room was the second or third floor of the tower, there were none of the facilities we have today, but otherwise things were much the same as they are now on the track, but without the chicanes at

48

Acque Minerali, at the top of the hill, or before the last corner. It was a very quick circuit.

"I remember it well from the F2 days, too. I think they used to have a double-header with a 2-litre sportscar race, and then the following week they'd have the Formula Two race, before we'd all drive off to Enna and do the same thing."

The F2 cars were back the following year, for the ninth round of the European series, when Peter Gethin dominated the first heat in the Chevron B20, and Bob Wollek the second in his Brabham BT38.

In conjunction with former Chevron engineer Paul Owens (now a mainstay of engineering at Reynard), Gethin recalled: "I won the first heat and was running second or third in the second when the fuel gauge broke, all the fuel came out over me and I had to stop. Paul tells me he remembers it very well because I came in and gave him a terrible bollocking!

"I thought it was a pretty good circuit. Very fast, but challenging. Hilly, and interesting."

John Surtees did sufficient with a fourth and a third place in the second Matchbox Team Surtees TS10-Hart to clinch the overall win from Wollek, Niki Lauda, Andrea de Adamich, Graham Hill and Jody Scheckter. This was an immensely popular victory for Surtees in front of an adoring Italian crowd that had never forgotten his achievements for MV Agusta and Ferrari; fittingly, it was Big John's last race victory, on his penultimate appearance.

"It was quite satisfying," he said. "Mike [Hailwood] was there as well, when we were running the little Hart engines. I'd semi-retired some time earlier because by then I only drove in what we then considered as development races. In many ways, perhaps earlier on I should just have concentrated on driving, but the team was growing and I had to spend more time being a jack of all trades. People kept telling me to delegate, but to delegate you have to pay the people, and if you haven't got the budget you end up where you can't delegate! I went along and did a drive where we thought a bit of development work was needed."

Surtees always enjoyed racing in Italy. "Perhaps Imola was less frantic than Monza, but it's a whole different region there. Different, but again superb food is available in the area, and there's a lot of enthusiasm. The enthusiasm was always immense in Italy. Where Monza was always Milan, Imola was Bologna, a very nice setting and a different region that was always restricted by the park rules, so you found practice was limited because of the times they could use the circuit. But they were always an enthusiastic bunch, and somewhat more relaxed than the hierarchy at Monza, who were a bit officious."

The sense of easiness and *camaraderie* drew the racers together in those days. "We had no motorhomes," Hutchinson recalled, "and I used to have a Volkswagen camper, known as Hotel Hutch. I used to park it against the back concrete wall in the paddock, and all the teams would be in a hotch-potch in the paddock. Between the heats, all the drivers, particularly the English drivers, would come along and we'd all brew up a cup of tea. I'd get everything that had happened in the race brought to me at Hotel Hutch because it was the only place you could get a decent cuppa! There was no catering at Imola at all, so my van became a sort of gathering centre. I've still got a guest book that all the drivers used to sign at Hotel Hutch. There were all sorts of people around in those days. If I remember right, the press officer then was Signor Belanda, who only had one front tooth; we used to call him Central Eating..."

Formula Two never returned to Imola, preferring Monza, Vallelunga, Misano and Enna-Pergusa, but over the ensuing years the track would stage a race for the World Championship for Sportscars, and further rounds of the Interserie, European GT and European 2-litre Sportscar Championships.

In May 1972 Willi Kauhsen had taken his Porsche 917-10 to victory over Helmut Kelleners' big McLaren M8F, Ernst Kraus' Porsche 917 Spyder and Nanni Galli's rather breathless Alfa Romeo T33TT/3, though Helmut Marko was the star. After mechanical problems in the first heat, the Austrian brought his BRM P167-Chevrolet home first in the second, his best lap of 1m 27.7s establishing a new lap record of 127.99mph that the F2 cars would not get close to when they raced in July. Two months later the rising Marko's career in topline motorsport was ended cruelly when he was blinded in his left eye by a flying stone when his BRM was running sixth, right behind Emerson Fittipaldi's Lotus 72, during the French GP at Clermont-Ferrand. Ironically, it had been Marko's best-ever showing in an F1 car.

At the end of the 1972 season Marko's efforts had placed Imola within the elite of the world's fastest road courses. Spa was quickest of them all at 157mph, followed by Monza at 153, Le Mans and the Osterreichring at 134, Silverstone at 133, Imola, and then Hockenheim at 126. Outside Europe, only Riverside, in California, and Donnybrook, in Minnesota, got close at 126 and 122 respectively.

Impressive though this was, its implications did not escape the circuit owners, and for 1973 modifications were implemented to slow things down. That's when the *Variante Alta* chicane came into being at the top of the hill, between *Acque Minerali* and *Rivazza*.

By now the circuit had already been renamed in honour of Dino Ferrari, and in 1972 an important political milestone had been reached when the town of Imola held a referendum whether to continue with the race track run by the Imola Sport and Tourist Association (ESTI), which had been in charge since the start, or to turn the operation over to the Automobile Club of Bologna to run things in association with a holding company,

Sagis. The referendum went in favour of the latter course, which promised better funding and greater professionalism on a full-time basis. Sagis would pay the town of Imola an annual rent and then take over the entire running of events at the circuit. Subsequently, each time a new deal was struck with FOCA, a deal of similar duration would be forged with the municipality. Thus began a new chapter under the continued guidance of Luciano Conti and his staff.

Conti is an interesting character. Besides running the Automobile Club of Bologna in his early days, he had also been president of the Scuderia Neptuno. "And," Franco Lini recounted, "Ferrari was pushing him to make a newspaper, a magazine. Ferrari liked something to express himself, and he didn't want to pay! So he invited Conti to make *Autosprint*. In 1964, 1965 it was a monthly magazine, and finally from 1966 it became a weekly. Ferrari liked to have a publication in which to make his opinion. If he wanted to say something he could, but he didn't want to pay to do it!"

Later, illness would force Conti to step down, and his place as president of Sagis would be taken over by lawyer Federico Bendinelli, but an exemplary press service at the Grand Prix would continue to be run by Gianni Berti.

When Kauhsen dominated both Interserie heats of the Shell Gold Cup on May 1, reigning CanAm champion George Follmer made a rare appearance in a similar car and set fastest lap in 1m 34.9s, a truncated average of 'only' 120.73mph for the revised track.

The World Championship for Sportscars made two visits to the *Autodromo Dino Ferrari*. In the 1,000kms event in 1974, Henri Pescarolo and Gerard Larrousse, sharing a Matra MS670C, finished two clear laps ahead of the *tifosi* favourites Rolf Stommelen and Carlos Reutemann in an Alfa Romeo 33TT12, with de Adamich and Carlo Facetti another seven laps adrift. In 1976 the *500km di Imola* comprised the third round of the series and was to be run as the *Trofeo Ignazio Giunti*, honouring the memory of the talented Roman, whose promising career had been ended when he crashed into Jean-Pierre Beltoise's almost stationary Matra as the Frenchman tried to push it back to the pits during the 1971 1,000kms race in Buenos Aires.

In battle with Porsche and Alfa Romeo for the championship, Renault entered a brace of its turbocharged Alpine-Renaults for Jean-Pierre Jarier and Jacques Laffite, and Jody Scheckter and Pescarolo. Porsche had a 936 for Jacky Ickx and Jochen Mass, and Alfa Romeo débuted its new T33S monocoque car for Arturo Merzario and Vittorio Brambilla.

There were to be a couple of dramatic incidents in the race that would serve as an indication of the underlying weakness of the entry list, and there had already been unpleasantness in qualifying, which befell Pescarolo. Shortly after Scheckter had set a time of 1m 43.21s, Pesca slid off the road at the first chicane in what appeared to be a minor moment. However, he was struck by a catchfence pole and knocked unconscious. Ask some *anciennes pilotes* about past incidents in their careers and they struggle with recall, but Pescarolo needed no prompting to call up that day, although ironically part of it has forever been eliminated from his memory bank.

"I remember this day, because I was unconscious, but I was able to help myself from the car! I went in the braking in the area of the chicane, and I think somebody had already gone off and thrown dust or sand or something on the track. I was trying to make my qualifying time and suddenly there was no more braking because it was very slippery. I thought it was no problem, because it was not so fast going into the escape area, but they had the fences with the poles, and I think I was hit in the face by one of these poles.

"People explain me that I got out of my car. That's what they said, but I don't know. The last thing I remember was when I missed my braking. After that it's a big hole. I don't remember anything until in the evening. People told me that I walked myself down to the pits or somewhere, I don't know, and they took me to the medical centre at the track, and I don't remember anything during three hours. My wife was there, and progressively I recognized her and I asked her what I was doing, where I was. In my life I have a big hole of three hours, where I don't remember anything. But I had no problem after that, and I raced the next day."

Later that day Merzario had a nasty scare when he saw flames in the mirrors of his new Alfa, which he deliberately spun at *Tosa* and vacated with alacrity; a fuel system leak was blamed.

Though 29 cars were entered, only four of them had serious status, the Porsche, both Alpines and the Alfa; the rest were mainly Italian-series makeweights. Jarier led from Scheckter initially, followed by Brambilla and Ickx. Scheckter retired early with a blown engine, however, leaving Ickx and Brambilla to provide the interest as Jarier disappeared into the distance. Just after quarter-distance the Alfa began to experience gear selection problems, but then Jarier tripped over Teodorico Zeccoli's ageing Alfa Romeo 33TT V8, which the Italian veteran was attempting to drive solo. 'Jumper' spun wildly – trackside observers suggested he may have rotated more than 10 times! – before crawling back to the pits to hand over to Laffite with a set of seriously flat-spotted Michelins. Their minute lead was erased, and Jacques resumed a lap and as much behind Ickx.

The two Frenchmen gradually unlapped themselves and began to make inroads into the Porsche's lead until it was Laffite's turn to stumble over a backmarker. In the chicane before the pits he came upon the bumbling Rodolfo Cescato, who was sharing a Sauber C5 with Herbie Muller. The two cars touched side-by-side, and though Jacques continued, a damaged water radiator had gone undetected, and when the Alpine's Renault V6 seized Ickx and Mass were left with a clear run to the flag, four laps ahead of Merzario and Brambilla in the Alfa 33TS3, and Jurgen Barth, Horst Godel and Reinhold Joest in their elderly Porsche 908/3.

For all his lost hours there, Pescarolo stills looks back fondly on Imola. "It was a circuit that I liked very much. There were very fast parts and, as you know, I always liked very fast tracks like Spa, Nurburgring and Clermont-Ferrand. And Imola was a track on which I was always very pleased to race because it was fast, technical and always interesting to drive." He firmly believed that the aim to create a small Nurburgring had been realized.

"Yes! It was a very, very mini Nurburgring. I think they found the right way to use the natural area, which they were not able to do on the new Nurburgring. It should have been possible to do something fantastic there, but it is just a shit track. No interest at all. But Imola, like Spa, has been able to do something interesting.

"I think the hairpin was a demanding corner, but all the track was quite interesting, because between all the corners you were at high speed, and with not too many chicanes like now. Interesting places to negotiate. There was not one place better than another; all the corners were good. To do a quick time on the track was interesting all the way round."

Andrea de Adamich shared Pescarolo's enthusiasm for Imola, and still holds the races he did there in the Alfa Romeo T33 sportscar as his favourites. "With the eight-cylinder TT cars it was tremendous fun, and because it was the quickest car I drove there, the more Nurburgring feeling you had from the circuit. With Formula Three certain corners were flat-out; but with the 3-litre Alfa, no. That was increasing the feelings and the satisfaction of the driving.

"The other thing is that the geography of the circuit for the public is the same, because the corners changed inside the circuit. Like Spa, they didn't change the concept. It is the same situation as today. Of course, in my day Ferrari was not so present in non-Formula One races, but the people were coming there even then, at Formula Three races, with their Ferrari flags, because of the region, where the concept was Ferrari."

If the *Trofeo Ignazio Giunti* had been a sorry tribute to one of Italy's most promising drivers, it did leave an important legacy. Having got the taste for international events, Imola began to look towards a time when Ferrari might indeed race his cars at the track, at the possibility of running its own Formula One race once more. The wheel had gone full-circle, and a new future beckoned.

WHY JODY DROVE FOR RENAULT

Jody Scheckter's presence in a Renault sportscar in the 1976 1,000kms endurance race fuelled speculation about an alliance between his current employer, Ken Tyrrell, and the French manufacturer for Formula One in 1977. But the reason was far more prosaic.

"Gerard Larrousse had suspended Patrick Depailler for a race for clashing with his team-mate Jean-Pierre Jarier at the Nurburgring, and Renault needed another driver just for Imola," explained Jabby Crombac. "They wanted an Elf driver, and that happened to be Scheckter.

"It had nothing to do with Tyrrell and Renault. In fact, that had all been got out of the way much earlier. Renault had offered Tyrrell the very first turbocharged Formula One engine and Tyrrell had said 'No' after thinking about it. But if you remember, when the Tyrrell six-wheeler first appeared at the end of 1975 it was blue, but had a yellow stripe that nobody understood. That stripe was for Renault, just in case Ken did the deal...!"

4
And Bernie helped too...

"We all dived in, including Bernie. He was underneath, passing the spanners." – Herbie Blash.

Following the tragedy at Monza in 1978, which had ultimately claimed the life of the enormously popular Ronnie Peterson, an anti-Monza feeling pervaded Formula One circles towards the end of the Seventies, and when it was announced that Imola was to stage a non-championship Formula One race on September 16, 1979, it soon became apparent that this was scheduled as a prelude to the Italian Grand Prix itself being held at Imola in 1980. This first *Gran Premio Dino Ferrari di F1* was held one week after the Italian Grand Prix at Monza, while the circus was still in Italy, and there was inevitable speculation that the circuit close to Bologna might be shaping up to provide permanent competition to the traditional home of Italy's most prestigious race.

There was no disputing that Imola was a popular enough site, but even so the decision to stage this initial race still came as something of a surprise to the motorsport world.

Initial reactions were mixed when the Ferrari, Brabham, Lotus, Arrows, Tyrrell, Alfa Romeo, Shadow, McLaren, Copersucar, Wolf, Merzario and Agostini Williams teams set up camp. Generally, the drivers liked the layout of the track, but as ever they were worried about safety. Imola had not really been affected too much by the various safety crusades of the Sixties, and although there had been some sizeable investment to update its facilities, it was still deemed to have several shortcomings.

Niki Lauda and Jody Scheckter completed a tour of inspection and identified several corners where drivers risked head-on accidents with concrete walls. They were also perturbed at the lack of sensible run-off areas at some of the faster corners, especially *Tamburello*. The latter point would haunt the organizers right up until the tragedies of 1994.

A token attempt was made to comply with some of Lauda's and Scheckter's more easily satisfied comments prior to the race, but there was still general consternation when a Renault 5 went off in one of the supporting races and flattened a section of Armco barrier whose mounting bolts appeared to be loose. The pits were considered to be totally unsuitable, and they were only part-finished. There was a general consensus, therefore, amongst those present that it was a good job that this was a 'prototype' race, and not the Italian Grand Prix itself.

Yet despite such misgivings, there was an end-of-term feeling to the meeting, which took place in a relaxed atmosphere. There hadn't been a Formula One race at Imola since 1963, of course, but Carlos Reutemann had done some tyre testing there for Michelin and Ferrari in late 1976, while Jean-Pierre Jarier had provided a bogey time to aim for with his sportscar lap record of 1m 42.3s (109.332mph), set in 1976 in the Alpine-Renault A442, and on that occasion he had taken pole position in 1m 40.23s.

When the Formula One cars took to the track again the Frenchman himself soon cut all previous marks to ribbons in his Tyrrell, slicing down to 1m 35.639s, despite a sticking skirt, but it was Gilles Villeneuve in the *tifosi*'s beloved Ferrari who was totally dominant in qualifying, taking pole position in his T4 with lap in 1m 32.91s, ahead of team-mate Jody on 1m 33.23s. Reutemann was third in the sole Martini Lotus 79 at 1m 33.94s, a second behind Gilles, and Lauda was fourth with 1m 34.80s in the V12 Alfa Romeo-engined Brabham BT48, almost another second adrift. It was the *tifosi*'s perfect front row.

Scheckter had clinched the World Championship the previous week and he confessed to the organizers that they needn't expect too much from him because he didn't feel in that much of a hurry to shine, but later he added: "Once you're in the cockpit you forget about driving slowly and try as hard as usual. It's something you have to do; you forget everything else..."

Patrese made the third row for Arrows along with Vittorio Brambilla, who was having what should have been his last outing for Alfa Romeo in Formula One. After Rosberg and Jarier on row four it was a pretty weak field, and there were just 16 cars in all. Bruno Giacomelli was 11th, setting the time in the old flat-12 Alfa after his new V12 developed serious oil system maladies. Shadow had rented a DN9 to Beppe Gabbiani, whose £15,000 outlay went up in the smoke that issued from his Ford DFV engine after he had damaged an oil pipe by going over a kerb, while team-mate Elio de Angelis (who would shine in later races at Imola) was back in 14th place, his engine blowing up after only two laps. Patrick Tambay (another man of Imola's future) was on the back row with no time recorded, after endless dramas with his McLaren, which blew its DFV in the morning and wasn't ready in time for afternoon qualifying.

The weather had been glorious for the previous two days, but raceday dawned grey and dull, and a steady downpour kept the *tifosi* in the warmth of their homes. The fact that the organizers had also arranged their race on the day when Bologna was playing Juventas might also have helped to account for the disappointing crowd.

Fortunately, the rain had stopped by the 10am warm-up and the track was dry enough for slicks by the end of the half-hour session, and by the 3.15pm start, the sun was back in command. It was pretty warm down at Brabham, too, for Lauda had blown his Alfa V12 that morning and all hands were required to replace it. The problem was, there weren't that many of them.

"Monza had been our last official Grand Prix with Alfa Romeo," recalled Herbie Blash, who then ran the Brabham team. "Basically, the whole team was shooting back to build the BT49, which was the Ford-engined car which would be going off to Canada and the United States for the final two races of the year. With me there in Imola were Chris Robson, maybe Charlie Whiting and one other mechanic. We were turning up, mainly, for our sponsor, Parmalat. It was a one-car effort, the lowest-key Formula One effort in years. We didn't have any engineers there; I was the engineer!

"When we blew the engine on race morning, we had a mad panic to change it in time for the race. We all dived in, including Bernie. He was underneath, passing the spanners. I remember him trying to put the nuts on the exhausts. We just got the car finished in time and then, lo and behold, we went out and won! It was against all odds. We should never have won, there was no way we should have won it!"

Ecclestone himself confessed that he didn't specifically recollect the incident, but said with a laugh: "If Herbie says I did it, then I did. It's unlikely, but I might have done. Who knows with me..."

Villeneuve had duly fulfilled the expectations of the *tifosi* and taken the early lead from Scheckter on the opening lap, and the two Ferraris led Reutemann and Lauda past the pits at the end of it, followed by Brambilla, Giacomelli, Patrese, Rosberg, Jarier, Agostini, Ribiero, de Angelis and Tambay. The lap-charters were not to be overtaxed. Giacomelli's race lasted for only four laps before he cruised into the pits. According to the rotund team boss Carlo Chiti a damaged radiator had arrested the progress of his new baby, but sceptics pointed to the pool of oil beneath the car and quickly formed their own opinions!

While the Ferraris remained just out of reach, Lauda passed Reutemann into third place on lap 10 after the Lotus had lost a wheel balance weight. Then, as the fuel loads lightened, the Italian cars began to slide around and destroy their rear tyres. Lauda passed Scheckter on lap 15, and the newly crowned World Champion conceded the place without demur.

Five laps later Niki pounced on Gilles, too, but this time he met the sort of stern opposition he would have expected of a man he rated very highly. Going down to *Tosa* on lap 21, 'The Rat' had taken the lead, but as he braked in the middle of the track Gilles came piling down the inside to regain the initiative. On the next lap Lauda overtook on maximum speed once again, and this time he kept the door closed at *Tosa*, where Villeneuve, also looking at the tight line again, had to brake harder than he expected. As he looked for room that wasn't there, the French-Canadian ran into the back of the Brabham. With the Ferrari's front wing knocked askew, Gilles dived into the pits for a replacement and some much-needed new tyres at the end of the lap, but though he would launch his customary charge through the field to an eventual seventh place, the race was all but over.

Reutemann was not having one of his glittering days, and was subdued by a soft brake pedal, so he never offered any real challenge to Lauda, who ran out an easy winner by a little under 19 seconds. Jody disappointed the crowd with an unspectacular third place from Riccardo Patrese, with Jarier and Rosberg filling out the top six.

There had been a little pantomime on the 17th lap that typified Brambilla's character as he and de Angelis collided while fighting over territory. Elio spun and stalled, his race ending there and then; Vittorio, however, kept his engine running and got back on to the track. As he drove away, two fingers emerged from the cockpit to comfort his frustrated rival...

As a new Formula One race it was scarcely inspiring, a feeling that was reflected in Lauda's haste to change into civvies. Moments after stepping on to the victory podium he was whisked away in Ecclestone's helicopter. The next race was in Canada, where he was destined to walk away from Formula One for the first time, abruptly turning his back on it during first practice and leaving the team with the task of finding a replacement in double-quick time. Had Bernie known what his team leader would do when he suddenly realized that he longer enjoyed "driving round in circles," as he put it, Lauda would almost certainly have had to make his own way out of Imola...

Despite the low-key overture the previous year, 1980 finally saw the realization of the big dream when Imola hosted the Italian Grand Prix. The politics behind the decision to abandon Monza that year were complex and far-reaching, but the overall decision had been thrashed out by three men: Bernie Ecclestone, Enzo Ferrari and Luciano Conti.

Though Monza had duly carried out the safety modifications demanded in the wake of Ronnie Peterson's death (which resulted not so much from his accident but from fat embollism associated with his broken legs), FISA and FOCA had already given their word that Imola could have the 1980 date. The 1979 non-championship race had been Imola's way of playing by the rule book, which at that time specified that venues aspiring to run a World Championship Grand Prix had first to stage a similar race during in the previous season before a licence would be granted; now it was the authorities' turn to honour a deal.

As in 1979, there were still a number of reservations about various aspects of the circuit, especially concerning run-off areas. The two existing chicanes, at *Variante Alta* and the last corner, were deemed okay, however, but somehow Jean-Pierre Jabouille and, of all people, Gilles Villeneuve had come up with a first-gear disaster at *Acque Minerali*, which was universally panned. It was a very silly affair, tight enough almost to double back on itself, and it demanded very heavy braking from *Piratella*. It was so narrow that it allowed only one car through at a time.

Elsewhere, the organizers had done an excellent job and they sprung a major surprise by creating a pit facility that was quickly dubbed the best in the world and which, in the judgment of the teams and press, bettered even that of the yardstick circuit, Paul Ricard. The garages were spacious and fully equipped with electricity and hydraulic lifting apparatus, and above them a mezzanine level housed a new press room, viewing suites for sponsors, a bank (still, oddly enough, a rarity at Formula One tracks), toilets (albeit French-style, where somebody had decided to economize by deleting the seats!) and a restaurant, which did brisk trade in *espresso*, *vino rosso* and crunchy bread rolls.

The paddock, too, was large enough to accommodate everybody, and the surface was fully tarmacadamed. Further down past the pits, a fully-equipped medical centre had been established.

This was all a very long way from the days of Hotel Hutch and Central Eating, and it made Monza look like Snetterton on a bad day. The Formula One world was impressed and delighted, and it would not be the last time that Sagis indicated its willingness to make very significant investment in its circuit when the necessity arose.

The town of Imola had never seen anything quite like it. The previous year's non-championship race had brought the *tifosi* to a frenzy of expectation (even though race day itself had been a disappointment), but this was something else, this was the Italian Grand Prix; Monza's race had come to Imola!

With a full-blown World Championship Grand Prix on the doorstep, it was no surprise that the town itself was *en fete*, full of the buzz, with Italian flags and Ferrari banners hanging from every building, and a seemingly permanent traffic jam that began on the Wednesday and didn't disperse until late into the Sunday evening. The chaos in the town would probably have caused an outrage anywhere else, certainly in Britain, but the people of Imola, even those who had never been to a motor race and probably didn't know a Ferrari from a fire engine [and there are rumoured to be one or two such people, even in Italy], all entered into the carnival mood and offered a warm welcome to motor racing's most prestigious travelling circus.

Each day, getting to the paddock on time became a test of dexterity and ingenuity, and the press room would be full of stories of passing hordes of banner-waving *tifosi* with their portable 'grandstands' and collapsible contraptions designed to improve their view of the track and their beloved Ferraris.

But when it came to qualifying time, it was the turbocharged Renaults, as usual, who were rampant, Rene Arnoux just shading Jean-Pierre Jabouille by half a second to claim pole position. Carlos Reutemann put his Williams on the second row, with Bruno Giacomelli's Alfa for company, ahead of Nelson Piquet's Brabham and Alan Jones' Williams. Villeneuve had tried Ferrari's new chunky-looking 126C turbo on the Saturday, and sent the tifosi into raptures with eighth fastest time before a turbocharger blew. But the car had serious throttle-lag problems and the computerized fuel injection clearly was a long way from perfect, while the first indications that this car might not be the panacea Maranello had sought came when Gilles let it slip that the handling was "slightly better than the T5," which at that time was a mere shadow of the previous year's Championship-winning T4.

Gilles took his grid slot with the 126C's time, but started the race in a normally aspirated 12-cylinder T5 as the new car was taken away for further development work. To mark the importance of the first Grand Prix at Imola, *Il Drake* himself was in attendance, but there was precious little for him to cheer, Scheckter already being detuned after a massive practice accident on the run down to *Tosa* on Saturday afternoon.

At close to maximum speed Jody had lost control of the T5, which spun backwards into the barriers. The right-hand side of the Ferrari was destroyed, and though he later took over the spare car it was hardly surprising that he did not better his 16th fastest time. All this had left the World Champion badly bruised and in no mood to do anything but plug home to the finish in the race. He had to use a special brace to support his injured neck, and he would finish a lowly eighth after a non-stop run.

Gilles, however, was his customary lightning bolt self as he blasted the hapless T5 into an initial fourth place before sustaining the puncture that, as we shall see, threw him off course at the corner that forever after would bear his name.

Piquet, meanwhile, had limbered up by winning Saturday's BMW Procar supporting race, and the Brazilian then simply blew the doors off the Renaults in the Grand Prix as the sun blazed down on the 120,000 spectators who had crammed into the autodrome in the hope of seeing a Ferrari victory.

Instead of making vain attempts to beat the turbo cars in qualifying, Piquet and Brabham designer Gordon Murray had opted instead to perfect their race set-up, and as a result of that wisdom Nelson was really flying. Whereas Carlos burned out his clutch trying to take the fight to the Renaults off the line, Nelson sat happily in third place until he passed Arnoux on the third lap, and then he took the lead from Jabouille a lap later. From then on he ran his own race and emerged a clear victor, delighting in rubbing it in with a 29-second margin over arch-rival Jones in the second Williams.

Villeneuve's accident was bad news for Giacomelli, who was holding his Alfa Romeo in fifth place, still right on the T5's tail after having been overtaken by Gilles on the previous lap. He had to retire after running over debris from the accident, which also gave the following Didier Pironi and Jean-Pierre Jarier nasty frights as the Ferrari slid back on to the track right in front of them.

The real interest had then centred on Jones' determined – and ultimately successful – pursuit of the Renaults, the Australian depriving Arnoux of third place on lap 12 as his brakes faded, and then Jabouille of second place just before the halfway mark. Further back, Reutemann was making amends for his startline exuberance with the clutch, which had now recovered enough to let him stage a brilliant recovery from last place.

By the 40th of the 60 laps the Italian Grand Prix was turning into something of a procession, and Renault could only groan as yet again its practice promise evaporated. Mario Andretti was on the verge of taking fourth place from Arnoux when his Lotus broke its Ford DFV engine, then Rene came under massive pressure from Jarier's Tyrrell. The former Shadow star finally squeezed by after a terrific effort – only to spin immediately afterwards as his brakes faded.

Reutemann sped through into fourth place in the melee, and as Arnoux dropped back to 10th in a Renault whose handling was rendered ever more erratic by a detached rear damper, Jabouille also ran into trouble. Everyone else behind Piquet and Jones moved up a place when the yellow and white car came to a halt with a broken gearbox with seven laps to go, just one before Jarier gave up the battle against his brakes.

Reutemann thus wound up in third place, despite being last at the end of the first lap, while Elio de Angelis, Keke Rosberg and Pironi completed the top six.

All this action going on at the front tended to obscure an early indication of what the future might hold, but at the back of the field a rookie Frenchman called Alain Prost had qualified his McLaren in last place on the grid, alongside Marc Surer's ATS, and he would bring it home unobtrusively in seventh place, while the first non-qualifier was the Lotus 81B driven by a determined Englishman called Nigel Mansell... The latter had gone off the road in trying to make way for a Ligier, and later, when he ran out of fuel, the marshals prevented his mechanics from helping him to get the stricken car going again. Both men, however, were destined to make quite an impact at Imola and elsewhere in the future.

In the meantime, Piquet's great victory was sufficient to give him a single-point lead over Jones in an increasingly hard-fought Championship clash, by 54 points to 53, with only two races – the Canadian and USA-East Grands Prix – left. But despite this defeat, Jones would win the title, although Piquet's time would come.

So Imola had staged its first World Championship Grand Prix for cars, and it had been a roaring success, but the deal had always been that the Italian Grand Prix would return to Monza for 1981. Plans were afoot, however, to ensure that Italy would stage a second Grand Prix each year. Fertile minds had already envisaged a San Marino Grand Prix at Imola...

A MIRACLE FOR GILLES

The gods make their own rules for life, and after the miracle that saved Gilles Villeneuve's when he crashed on the fifth lap of the 1980 Italian Grand Prix, it was sadly ironic that Roland Ratzenberger would later lose his when he lost control of his infinitely stronger Simtek S941 at the same spot 14 years later.

From eighth on the grid, Gilles was in fourth place, fighting in the wake of the Renaults and Piquet's Brabham, when as he swept down to *Tosa* on lap five his right rear tyre exploded at maximum velocity. He went off the road at unabated speed at the point where the straight begins to curve right on the rush down to the hairpin, and he instantly became a passenger in the hands of destiny.

"As I went into the corner I was suddenly aware of a 'thump-thump' from one of the rear wheels," he told Alan Henry of *Motoring News*. "I was just registering "A tyre's coming off" when the car went away from me. That was quite something, I can tell you. I thought that I was really going to hurt my legs in this one..."

Three hours after the accident, Henry came across the French-Canadian calmly strolling through the paddock, accompanied by his wife Joanne and their children Jacques (now Damon Hill's partner at Williams) and Melanie, and without being blasé his cool description of the incident portrayed graphically how aware he was of his miraculous deliverance.

"As I hit the bank on the left, the left front wheel came up and the rim caught me full in the face," he recalled, in a comment made all the more chilling from the perspective of 1994. "I now realize my helmet was cracked. The car shot back across the road. When it came to a halt, I opened my eyes and I couldn't see. I could hear cars going by, but I wasn't sure where I was. That's why I stayed in the car for a few moments. After half a minute or so my vision came back and I could see okay. I was pretty worried, I can tell you."

Worried enough, he confided later to *Autosport*'s Nigel Roebuck, to believe momentarily that he had gone blind.

"That Ferrari T5 is remarkably strong," Gilles continued to Henry.

"You'd be surprised just how little distortion of the cockpit took place. That was a big shunt, but it stood up pretty well. I'm a bit stiff and I'm sure I'll be bruised tomorrow. My helicopter? Yes, I'll be flying home to Monaco if I'm okay in the morning. But I'll be taking someone else along with me to help with the flying..."

He paused, and then a big smile spread across his face.

"You know, the really funny thing about the accident was that I was taking it easy. I really was. I wanted to finish without a stop for fresh tyres. The car was going really well!"

SADNESS FOR ALFA

Tragedy struck the Alfa Romeo team on the Friday before the race when a helicopter carrying team personnel overturned on landing at the circuit. Designer Carlo Chiti was unhurt in the incident, but an engineer and two mechanics were injured and one of the latter succumbed to his injuries in hospital in Imola on Sunday evening.

Number two driver Vittorio Brambilla had already crashed his road car *en route* to the track on that Friday morning, but was unharmed, and then he spun out of his last Formula One race on the fourth lap, becoming the first retirement. The 'Monza Gorilla', as he was affectionately named by peers who sometimes questioned his trackcraft, had been involved in the accident at Monza at the start of the 1978 Italian Grand Prix when his Surtees hit the barriers in the mêlée involving Ronnie Peterson. He sustained serious head injuries, and though he recovered, he never again reached the level that had taken him to victory in the rain during the 1975 Austrian Grand Prix.

At Imola it was left to team-mate Bruno Giacomelli to boost the team's battered morale with the third fastest practice time that Friday, and though he slipped to fourth in the final order on Saturday he pushed very hard in the early stages of the race. He was running fourth until Villeneuve pushed by, and then sadly his Alfa 179 sustained a puncture and suspension damage after running over debris as the Ferrari crashed right in front of him on lap five. He was thus the race's second retirement.

5
Skirting the issue

"If one does not clean it up, Formula One will end up in a quagmire of plagiarism, chicanery and petty rule interpretation forced by lobbies manipulated by people for whom the word sport has no meaning."
– Colin Chapman

Since Formula One had returned to Imola, the 1981 San Marino Grand Prix was to be the closest so far that Ferrari had come to victory, as Didier Pironi came within 13 tantalizing laps of the triumph that all of Italy craved. And though Nelson Piquet subsequently came from behind to rob the *tifosi* and ruin the script, this race was regarded as one of the best Formula One encounters in years and it laid the foundation for the newly instigated event's long-running success.

After the 1980 hiatus, the Italian Grand Prix had always been due to return to its spiritual home at Monza, but even as the cheers were fading for the event just held at Imola, plans were being hatched to allow Italy to stage not just its traditional World Championship encounter, but a second one as well: the normal Italian Grand Prix to be held at Monza and the second race to be run at Imola under the flag of the San Marino Principality. Effectively, it was a cunning scheme to duplicate the ruse that allowed France to have both the French and Monaco GPs.

It was a popular move as Imola's layout – and the general 'feel' and character of the region, with its intensely enthusiastic people and rolling green countryside – had greatly been enjoyed by the Formula One fraternity in the previous two years, once their initial reservations had been overcome. And the reward would be a cracking race.

Bernie Ecclestone was one of the prime-movers behind the deal, and he recalled: "It was myself, Mr Enzo Ferrari and Luciano Conti. It came out basically because Enzo wanted a race there, what with the circuit being called after his son, Dino. He asked me what the chances were of having a race there and we campaigned together, with Conti, and that's it. It was Enzo's idea to call it the San Marino Grand Prix. Quite clever, that..."

And so was Bernie's acumen in developing the race, for these were uneasy times between the teams allied to FISA, the governing body, and those represented by FOCA, the constructors' organization run under the presidency of Bernie, and it would do no harm at all to future causes if the strongest of the FISA *grandee* teams was in no small measure beholden to the man who led the upstart FOCA *garagistes*. There never have been any flies on Ecclestone when it comes to seeing wood rather than trees.

Thus the San Marino Grand Prix officially came into being for 1981, and the Imola event moved from its September slot in the calendar to early May, which would remain the tradition. Ecclestone had also shrewdly arranged that, more often than not, it would kick off the start of the European part of the Formula One season.

This time it was to be the fourth round of the World Championship, which had begun at Long Beach, California, in March, and provided World Champion Alan Jones with victory for Williams. The Didcot team had won again in Brazil a fortnight later, but this time Carlos Reutemann had decided to disobey team orders and stay ahead of Jones as they sped to the chequered flag in an easy 1-2 victory that had the beefy Australian seething with an undying hatred of the Argentinian star. This inter-team rivalry – which would later be made to look like little more than a kindergarten spat over who would use which spade in the sandpit once Senna and Prost hit their stride – would remain a factor throughout the season, and one which Nelson Piquet would shrewdly exploit as he headed towards the first of his three world titles.

The Brazilian had finally hit his top form in the third race, in Argentina, where Reutemann, of course, had most wanted to win; Piquet beat the local hero by 26 seconds. Jones, who finished a disgruntled fourth, was made all the more irritated by the evident level of competitiveness from his arch-rival at Brabham.

Piquet owed a decent slice of his victory to a clever hydro-pneumatic suspension system, which had been developed by designer Gordon Murray and was intended to regain much of the downforce which had been lost when the sliding plastic skirts, used the previous season beneath the sidepods to generate ground effect, had been banned for 1981. By using a system which lowered the ride height of the cars while they were on the move, Murray had become the first designer successfully to comply with the FISA requirement of a 6cm ground clearance which would be measured while cars were stationary, yet still allow his car to run a lot closer to the ground because the sidepods 'drooped' when it was in action and the gap could not be calculated by authority. The effectiveness of the system was not only proved when Piquet ran away and hid in Argentina, but also when journeyman racer Hector Rebaque, his team-mate, overtook Reutemann for second place at one stage as if the Argentinian was standing still. The Mexican eventually succumbed to rear suspension damage, but his performance had put the cat well and truly among the pigeons.

The circus came to Imola prepared for another needle-match between the two men thought most likely to be the main championship contenders, Piquet and Jones, and the scrutineers awaited them, armed with every rule book they could lay their hands on. For Brabham, in particular, it was going to be a bumpy ride.

Meanwhile, the *tifosi* was faithfully hoping for a strong Ferrari performance now that the ungainly 126C turbo cars were becoming a little better sorted. Gilles Villeneuve and Didier Pironi were not to disappoint them, though fortune would eventually swing the race away from the Prancing Horse.

Down in the paddock, the Toleman team quietly slipped into the Formula One maelstrom with its two bulky turbocharged cars for British drivers Brian Henton and Derek Warwick, who had run riot in Pirelli-shod Toleman Formula Two cars the previous season. The team would discover that Formula One was a markedly tougher nut to crack, however. Nevertheless, though neither driver would qualify – indeed, it would take the team until almost the end of the season before it scraped into a race – many admired Toleman's bold decision to go with Brian Hart's four-cylinder turbocharged engine, when simply bolting in customer Ford DFVs must have seemed quite an appealing alternative.

This refreshingly different approach was to be typical of the Toleman team, which would frequently demonstrate a reluctance to follow the herd. It was something of a maverick, thanks in great measure to the individual character and clear-sighted aims of managing director Alex Hawkridge, who had his own ideas of how to go about things. And although this Imola race would be a disappointment to the newcomer, it was part of the foundation of what eventually would be metamorphosed into the highly successful Benetton team.

That Friday in Imola, Formula One once again plumbed the depths of bad taste, the aggravation beginning in the scrutineering bay, where the organizers' men were taking their task very seriously indeed. Soon a massive argument had blown up over the interpretation of the word 'fixed'. The teams, which naturally chose to interpret things in whatever proved to be the most positive and, for them, beneficial light, said that 'fixed' did not mean that their static skirts could not be flexible. The scrutineers, however, took the view that 'fixed' meant 'rigid', *ie* unmoving. Thus the flexible, 'movable' skirts on the Williams, Brabham, McLaren, Tyrrell, Arrows, Ensign, ATS, Fittipaldi, Alfa Romeo, Osella and Theodore cars were declared not legal. Nor were any plastic seals betwixt rear tyres and sidepods, which nixed the same cars on a second count. And they didn't like the extensions to the front wing endplates on the Williams and the Tyrrells, either. And just in case Brabham had other ideas, they firmly rejected any form of hydro-pneumatic suspension...

There was complete uproar as accusations of favouritism for Ferrari and Renault began flying around. Initially Frank Williams was ecstatic to see the Brabhams' suspension outlawed, but then the senior FOCA teams sat down for a pow-wow on Friday morning as Ferrari, Renault, Alfa Romeo, March, Osella and Toleman got on with the job in untimed practice. There was a mood to abandon the race in some FOCA quarters, and then Williams and Ecclestone clashed very strongly over the question of hydro-pneumatics. As everything was delayed, the spectators sat cat-calling and waiting for the real action to start. By two o'clock, compromises had at last been thrashed out and, more than an hour late, the first official qualifying session finally got under way. Ecclestone had managed to beat out an agreement whereby hydro-pneumatic suspension was acceptable, but only with rigid skirts; FISA would issue a clarification of the meaning of 'fixed' in time for the next race, the Belgian Grand Prix at Zolder, a fortnight hence.

The FOCA teams had rather shot themselves in the foot with all this arguing, for when the session finally started the weather was cooler and the air was perfect for turbos, only Reutemann interloping in fourth place as Rene Arnoux, Gilles Villeneuve, Alain Prost and Didier Pironi staged a forced-induction *tour de force*.

Mercifully, out on the circuit the silly first-gear *Acque Minerali* chicane had been modified a little, so it was now less tight and cars could at least negotiate it in second gear. Meanwhile, all around the course the officials rather naïvely posted observers, whose hopeful function was to spot whether any car was running closer than 6cm to the ground. Quite how anyone actually hoped to prove this transient point was never fully explained, but then this was clearly developing into one of those weekends when Formula One's logic and credibility did not bear too close scrutiny.

Though the dissent among the rank and file of the FOCA teams continued into the second day – Jack Oliver of Arrows in particular felt that other teams had persuaded the scrutineers to interpret things in a manner that favoured them alone – the mood was generally lighter. And as the *tifosi* sensed that the dramatically increased competitiveness of the Ferraris was no flash in the pan, they cheered Villeneuve as, during the final moments of second qualifying, he clicked his own stopwatch on the pit wall to monitor his team-mate's progress in challenging the pole position lap of 1m 34.523s that he had set earlier.

The Ferraris were still very tricky to drive on the limit, despite their obvious power. Harvey Postlethwaite, now managing director of engineering at Tyrrell, but at that time charged with trying to make some sense of Ferrari's technical department, puts Gilles' spectacular performance into further perspective:

"That car, Ferrari's first turbo car... that chassis was the most dreadful thing you've ever seen. When I went there it was the most dastardly, dreadful chassis you've ever seen in your life! The engine was pretty good, but the chassis was a welded aluminium spaceframe with rivetted-on panels, when everyone else was just getting into carbon-fibre! They were probably 10 years behind at that point. We closed the gap pretty quickly, but... That car was an absolute dog, and that was the year when Gilles kept getting to the head of races and just sort of controlling a train, like he did in Spain, and then he won Monaco.

"If there were two right-hand or two left-hand corners one after the other, then you could get the car round them all right, but when you'd got a right-hand corner followed by a left, it didn't work at all because you had to get all the rivets loaded up the other way! It was the only monocoque that there's ever been a torsion test on where it had a genuine hysteresis point in the middle!"

There is slow-motion movie footage of Villeneuve putting the car through what was then the fast sweeping section down by the rowing basin in Montreal, later in that season, where you can actually see the thing pitching and weaving its way along like an evil high-speed crab. This, then, was the car with which Villeneuve and Pironi were obliged to wrestle again in front of the doting fans, and in which the French-Canadian lapped seven-tenths of a second faster than Arnoux's infinitely better behaved Renault RE20B.

The *tifosi* was in bubbling form that afternoon, cheering wildly whenever Didier drove past the pits in those final laps, and it had screamed itself hoarse when Gilles' heroic lap was announced. And, recognizing a sensational effort when they heard it, they also gave Reutemann due credit for a fantastic 1m 35.229s lap, which hoisted his Williams on to the front row alongside Gilles. With the Renaults of Rene Arnoux and Alain Prost on 1m 35.281s and 1m 35.579s respectively, that was territory where a normally aspirated car really had no right to be, especially as Piquet managed only 1m 35.733s and Jones' best was 1m 36.280s, more than a complete second adrift of his team-mate after a valve had dropped in his race car's DFV. This left him eighth fastest as Pironi's efforts had yielded him the sixth best time of 1m 35.868s, just ahead of John Watson's 1m 36.241s in the promising new carbon-fibre McLaren MP4/1. And the Australian, a perspirer at the best of times, was rather less than amused as he drove back into the pits, his face lobster red, to find Carlos already changed into civvies and calmly asking him whether he had had any problems. No, there was no love lost between those two...

For the *tifosi*, then, the climax to practice had been as exciting as the beginning had been anti-climactic, and as Formula One seemed to have sorted itself out again the one question that interested them was: Can the Ferraris win tomorrow?

In a repeat of 1979, two days of glorious practice weather gave way to pouring rain on the Sunday morning, but whereas it had dried out then, it remained wet this time, and although the rain had actually ceased as the grid formed, the track surface was still very slippery and the skies uncertain. Most drivers plumped for 'wet' tyres, but Rosberg, Tambay and Surer decided to gamble on slicks.

Villeneuve took the lead, as everyone knew he would, and the zealousness of officials witnessed in the scrutineering bay was not evident amongst those on the startline as Pironi introduced rolling starts to Formula One to grab second place from Reutemann by the time they reached *Tosa*. Two Ferraris in the lead! The *tifosi* screamed orgasmically.

Then, as if feelings were not already high enough between Reutemann and Jones, the Australian knocked his vulnerable nose wing askew on his team-mate's rear tyres in trying to barge through into third place on the plunge through *Piratella*, and the pit stop that was necessitated at the end of the lap damned his chances for the day, in conjunction with a further brace of tyre stops.

Prost lasted only three laps before retiring with gearbox trouble, and then Reutemann had a moment on lap six as he skated off the road exiting the second *Rivazza* and was nearly collected by Patrese. Piquet, meanwhile, took advantage of physical attacks on Arnoux, first by Watson and then by Jacques Laffite, to move ahead of the Renault into fifth place by lap seven. Gear selection difficulties and a wheel vibration would further ruin the Frenchman's day.

The Ferraris continued to dominate until Villeneuve pitted on lap 15, Gilles judging the moment right to switch to slicks since he had Jones' slick-shod Williams sitting right in his mirrors, one lap down after its early stop. Patrese thus rose to second place from Reutemann, whose Williams had developed a worrying vibration as his Michelins turned on their rims and went out of balance.

Pironi had immediately guessed what Gilles was up to as he saw his team-mate go into the pits, but he knew there was no point in following suit on that lap because of the crowded pit lane. He decided to stay out for another lap, and he felt the gift from the gods as it began to rain again. Villeneuve realized he'd been short-changed by Lady Luck as the track became slick again, and after falling to 13th he dropped another place with a further stop on lap 17, when he went back on to wets. By now all chance of victory for him had gone, but he managed to cling on to the lead lap. Pironi, therefore, was now the *tifosi*'s main hope.

Piquet pushed past Patrese for second place on lap 22, and now the Brazilian had a clear run to try to do something about Pironi's 10-second lead. He was untouched by two incidents, one in which Bruno Giacomelli and Eddie Cheever eliminated one another, the American claiming they had been running side-by-side, "literally eyeball-to-eyeball," when the

Italian had simply turned into him. Then Beppe Gabbiani brought to a halt the impressive Tyrrell debut of an up-and-coming Formula Three driver called Michele Alboreto, T-boning him at the *Tosa* hairpin in an ill-advised passing move. Exit both Tyrrells and both Osellas...

Now the race began to slip away from Ferrari, for in what some of the more imaginative *garagistes* might have seen as poetic justice, Pironi's car had broken a skirt, and as it yawed from lock to lock the increasing oversteer was taking its toll on its rear Michelins. Piquet was still advancing, although between them, running on slicks a lap down in the Theodore, Patrick Tambay was putting in the sort of performance he hadn't been able to summon since his debut days with Ensign in 1977.

The enormously popular Frenchman would do enough that day to lodge himself firmly in Ferrari minds, and when tragedy visited the team with Villeneuve's death at Zolder the following year, Patrick would be the man who got the call to duty. And a year after that he would avenge Gilles with an emotional success on this very course.

By lap 40, with 20 to run, Piquet was close enough to start challenging Pironi, but Didier used all of the Ferrari's turbo power to squirt out of reach every time the Brabham got close enough to come into the range of his peripheral vision. Meanwhile, further back, as Patrese continued to hold off Reutemann, Villeneuve was charging towards the points with a string of fastest laps.

The game of cat-and-mouse between Piquet and Pironi kept the crowd enthralled until a united gasp of anguish on the 47th lap signalled that the Ferrari had lost the lead. And as is so often the case once a driver loses his rhythm, Pironi found the Ferrari becoming slower and slower in the final stages as first Patrese, then Reutemann and finally Hector Rebaque, in the second Brabham, all slipped by to leave him a miserable fifth after a doughty performance. The never-say-die Villeneuve had risen as high as sixth, pounding along after Rebaque, but with two laps remaining a slipping clutch dropped him behind Andrea de Cesaris' McLaren, and finally Watson's recovery also swept him by the gritty Tambay to claim 10th place only a matter of yards from the flag.

In the end, then, Piquet and the nimble Brabham-Ford triumphed by five seconds over Patrese's Arrows, and seven over Reutemann's Williams, allowing Nelson to ease himself into second place in the World Championship standings, three points behind Carlos but four ahead of Jones.

And though the outcome was a bitter disappointment for the *tifosi* after the Ferraris had flattered so much, the very fact that both of them had finished was a pointer to future form, especially given Imola's reputation for placing a premium on fuel economy and seeking out mechanical weaknesses. It was further writing on the wall, however, for the anti-turbo brigade, which would soon have to pay very close attention to the words scrawled by their more potent rivals.

Meanwhile, after Piquet had won in style in Imola, the Brabham crew got a little more of its own back on officaldom when the teams went to Zolder, in Belgium, for the next Grand Prix. "We took the piss and had a bloody great lever that looked as if it raised and lowered the car!" chuckled Herbie Blash. "I suppose that was Alastair Caldwell's idea... Most things were, at least as far as he was concerned!" It was amusing, yes, but after the acrimony in qualifying at Imola it would take a while before Formula One could hold its head up again. Only the racing itself had saved the day in the first San Marino Grand Prix.

LOTUS DOESN'T SHOW

If Brabham in particular initially had reason to feel peeved in Imola, Lotus was feeling far more aggrieved back in Hethel following the FIA Court of Appeal's decision to ban the controversial Lotus 88.

As innovative as ever, Colin Chapman had come up with a means of having his technical cake and eating it; of creating a car that was very stiffly sprung and thus created consistent downforce, yet which insulated its drivers with a smooth ride. He did this by creating the twin-chassis concept, where he suspended the bodywork as a separate chassis on the main monocoque centre-section, which incorporated the suspension, wheels and running gear. This the FIA rejected, claiming that it did not conform to the regulations in its infamous and frequently ambiguous *Yellow Book*. Chapman would be at war over it for the first three races, after the car had initially been banned from the US Grand Prix (West) at Long Beach. After further farce in Brazil, things had reached a fresh crisis in Argentina where a furious Chapman left the country before practice had even started, leaving a strongly worded press statement in his wake.

Among many things, he wanted to reconsider his position, and "Whether Grand Prix racing is still what it purports to be: the pinnacle of sport and technological achievement." And he added trenchantly: "Unfortunately, this appears to be no longer the case and, if one does not clean it up, Formula One will end up in a quagmire of plagiarism, chicanery and petty rule interpretation forced by lobbies manipulated by people for whom the word sport has no meaning."

And he had added a cutting postscript: "When you read this, I shall be on my way to watch the progress of the US Space Shuttle, an achievement of human mankind which will refresh my mind from what I have been subjected to in the last four weeks."

This was all too much for the volatile FISA President Jean-Marie Balestre, who ostensibly was having a busman's holiday in Argentina. The voluble Frenchman immediately issued a statement claiming Chapman to be in breach of the Concorde Agreement [under the rules of which Grand Prix racing was staged], and for good measure threw in one of his famous off-the-cuff fines on the Lotus chief of $100,000.

However, he had reckoned without the rest of the Formula One paddock. Chapman's rivals might have been perfectly happy to see a car which potentially posed a very serious threat being prevented from racing, but they closed ranks as Balestre attempted to kick their colleague while he was down. Representatives of 13 teams signed a motion of censure on Balestre's comments and the fine, and shortly afterwards the show of strength saw the latter rescinded.

On April 23 the Court of Appeal ruled against the Lotus 88 in Paris, and by May 1, when practice began at Imola, the Lotus team was nowhere to be seen. Chapman had got by with the old Lotus 81s for the first three races, but now, faced finally with the need for something new in the wake of the 88's demise, had decided on April 28 that there was insufficient time to modify the newer cars to an acceptable standard.

There were other problems, too, because the enigmatic David Thieme, who sponsored Lotus via his Essex Petroleum business, and who had made many enemies in his time in Formula One, had been arrested in Zurich following a malpractice complaint lodged against him by a Swiss bank, Credit Suisse. The man who liked to effect the goatee beard and sherry-region hat of Zorro was later released on £70,000 bail, but these were edgy days for Chapman and Lotus, and Imola marked their first failure to take part in a Grand Prix since their debut at Monaco in 1958.

The only other time this ever happened would be at Spa-Francorchamps, eight years later, when neither Nelson Piquet nor Satoru Nakajima made the cut, but otherwise Lotus would never fail to get at least one car into a race until the team sadly folded at the beginning of 1995.

"I wish I could have taken this decision in better heart. I wish I could feel that I have had a reasoned discussion with a panel of open-minded persons who were competent to judge on the technicalities involved in the official language of the technical rules of the Concorde Agreement and of motor racing itself," said an embittered Chapman.

"And if to be proved wrong, then by logical argument drawn only from the letter and intent of the rules in force, presented in a coherent and comprehensive manner.

"So far, this has not happened, and when I eventually get a full statement as to the reasons advanced for this bizarre decision, then I may be willing to comment further."

Some say that Colin Chapman never fully recovered from the FIA's rejection of his clever new car, and that his faith in and love for Formula One was never the same again. That, when he died on December 16 a year later, a vital part of him had already succumbed.

Shortly after all this fiasco, I went on a trip to Daytona to see the Firecracker 400 NASCAR race, among other things. While I was there I did an interview with Big Bill France, the legend behind the Floridan track, and at one stage we talked of the Formula One scene. When I asked his opinion of the situation in general, and of the Lotus 88 ruling in particular, he rolled his eyes, laid his big farmboy hands on the desk, looked me straight in the eye, with a twinkle and a grin, and said: "Boy, it's all fucked up." They were my sentiments precisely.

6
Betrayal

"Finishing second is one thing... I would have been mad at myself for not being quick enough if he had beaten me. But finishing second because that bastard steals it... Jesus, that's why I'm mad!" – Gilles Villeneuve

Few races have started out with such apparently meagre chances of providing a spectacle – after all, a mere 14 cars were on the grid – yet have bucked the odds to produce something so gripping. And few have been run against such a backdrop of animosity as the 1982 San Marino Grand Prix. Fewer still have seen such animosity blown into insignificance by the controversy that surrounded their outcome, nor by such a tragic sequel. The *tifosi*, however, had already received a taste of things to come after the acrimony over the interpretation of technical rules that had soured practice on the Friday of the previous year's race.

In retrospect, of course, we know that this was to be Gilles Villeneuve's last race, and that makes it even less bearable that he should lose it in such a controversial manner.

These were troubled times for Formula One, for though the great war that had been brewing for months between FISA and FOCA had largely been averted after some close calls at the end of 1980, and at times during 1981, bad feeling remained everywhere, and the Formula One circus was still divided in its uneasy truce.

As I have indicated earlier, in the 'red' corner were the so-called *grandees*, the constructors such as Ferrari, Renault, Alfa Romeo, who had been joined by the newly emergent Toleman team, and who designed and built all of their cars, including – except for Toleman – the engine, and who were firmly aligned with FISA President Jean-Marie Balestre.

In the 'blue' corner stood Bernie Ecclestone, head of the Formula One Constructors' Association, and his massed troops of *garagistes*, as the *grandees* so disparagingly liked to refer to teams which made their own chassis but used proprietary power units. On the face of it, Toleman should have been a *garagiste* because it actually bought in its four-cylinder turbo engines from Brian Hart, but managing director Alex Hawkridge was his own man and had decided to align with the *grandees*.

This was not a war about the manner in which cars were built, however. It was something much deeper than that, a trial of strength to take control of the entire sport and the manner in which it was run. The French had always seen themselves as the true chiefs of motorsport, for hadn't they formed the rules since the year dot, via the FIA and the CSI? Didn't the ghost of Chevalier Rene de Knyff and the Automobile Club de France still stalk the hallowed portals of the FIA's opulent headquarters in the Place de la Concorde?

This, too, was the time when the *garagistes* were beginning to see that the writing on the wall, the writing that spelled the word turbo, was not just in capital letters, but was italicized, too. Since 1977 Renault had been struggling with the alternative concept of a 1.5-litre engine with turbocharging, which the rules had allowed for alongside the normally aspirated 3-litre engines that everybody else had chosen to use since the formula came into effect in 1966.

Since 1979 the Renault had been an occasional winner, and then Ferrari had also made the switch. The *garagistes* had countered the power of the turbo engines with superior chassis technology during the ground effects era, but the FIA had continuously campaigned against such devices as under-chassis skirts, and gradually the constructors had been losing ground. Superior handling had been compromised, yet the power of the turbo engines was increasing all the time, without any restrictions. The balance, they felt, was getting decidedly lop-sided.

Moreover, it was only a matter of time [it would happen that very season] before Gordon Murray's genius produced a really good-handling chassis to mate to a highly competitive turbo engine, in this case BMW's four-cylinder unit. This was also a time when an alliance with a major engine manufacturer was becoming ever more important, and those teams who had been brought up on the traditional British 'kit-car' way of going racing, and who did not have immediate or imminent access to a turbocharged power unit, were beginning to get extremely nervous and protective about the future. The face of Grand Prix racing was changing.

Some teams, notably Williams, had hit on a splendid wheeze to redress what they saw as an imbalance between the mandatory fighting weight of 500kg of all competing cars and the superior power of the turbo engines; they carried ballast in the form of water, ostensibly to cool their brakes. Of course, you would have needed a single-figure IQ to believe that this was necessary, and during the races the water was simply dumped. Hey presto, the cars now ran appreciably lighter than their turbo counterparts (which also needed more fuel), but could then be brought back up to the legal minimum weight afterwards by the simple expedient of replenishing the water reservoirs as part of the supposedly accepted practice of topping-up expendable fluids before the cars were weighed in the *parc ferme*.

Nelson Piquet's Brabham had won the Brazilian Grand Prix from Keke Rosberg's Williams, but since then their cars had been excluded for infringing the rules by running underweight; FISA had decided to get tough and close the loophole. FOCA said there was nothing specifically to prevent topping-up, and FISA said there was nothing specifically to allow it. And it was FISA's game.

Feeling that they had been backed into a corner, with no further means of appeal, Williams in particular had been a prime-mover behind the idea of a boycott of the San Marino Grand Prix, the plan being to show FISA that it couldn't stage a decent Formula One race without the FOCA teams.

To give an idea of how high feelings ran at this time, Frank Williams refused to speak to *Motoring News* reporter Alan Henry for six months after he had blown the cover of the water bottle story in print; Williams' normally affable and urbane colleague Charlie Crichton-Stuart steadfastly ignored him, while McLaren's Teddy Mayer had openly accused Henry and his *Autosport* opposite number Nigel Roebuck of being in the pay of Renault, simply because both had given equal space to the opposite side of the argument. Such can be the mental tensions of Formula One...

When the San Marino Grand Prix came around, feelings were at their most warlike, and Ecclestone duly decreed that the FOCA teams must boycott the event altogether, to teach FISA a lesson. Thus only 14 cars went to the grid; there were, of course, two Ferraris, to be driven by Gilles Villeneuve and Didier Pironi. Rene Arnoux and Alain Prost had their two Renaults, and Alfa Romeo brought along two cars for Bruno Giacomelli and the hot-headed youngster Andrea de Cesaris, who had been dropped by McLaren when Ron Dennis finally tired of rebuilding the cars he had damaged in 1981. Local team Osella had two cars, too, for Jean-Pierre Jarier and the ill-starred newcomer Riccardo Paletti, while Toleman entered Derek Warwick and Teo Fabi in its ugly but improving machines, and the irascible Gunther Schmid as usual did his own thing to bring two ATSs to the line for Manfred Winkelhock and Eliseo Salazar. These, then, were the FISA teams, but there were also two Tyrrells.

'Uncle Ken' had been obliged to break ranks with FOCA because of a newly inked sponsorship deal with Italian white goods manufacturer Candy, and of his ongoing alliance with Cooperativa Ceramica Imola; ever the pragmatist, he had done what he needed to do to keep his team going. But there would be a price.

The other FOCA teams stayed at home following a majority vote taken at a meeting in London on the Wednesday before the race; there was no sign of Williams, McLaren, Lotus, Arrows or Ensign or, naturally, Brabham. Williams went so far as to issue a release inviting members of the press to a conference at Didcot the Tuesday after the race. On one copy in the Imola press room, the outspoken *Motor Sport* doyen Denis Jenkinson had summed up the feelings of many with the scrawled words: 'If Frank Williams wants to talk to me, I'll be in the Zolder paddock.' Most felt Frank should have been in Imola to face the music and explain himself.

As things turned out, far from being a hollow race, the Grand Prix had all the hallmarks of great drama. Gerard 'Jabby' Crombac, that great reporter who has seen and noted more than most others have put together during his 500-odd races, said wryly: "That was a great defeat for FOCA, of course. Everybody expected a complete disaster, but Ferrari was there, that was enough. They had a fantastic race, a record crowd."

Not even Villeneuve could do anything about the Renaults in qualifying, his best lap being half a second slower than Prost's, who in turn was a similar amount off Arnoux. But in those days the reliability of the Renaults was still questionable.

In the Ferrari camp, the deal was that whichever of the two drivers was ahead of the other when the Renaults fell out would win the race. And therein lay the other factor that was to make this such an explosive – and ultimately fatal – duel.

A massive crowd crammed into the autodrome that Sunday and, confirming expectations, they watched Arnoux forge into a lead that he would maintain for the first 26 laps. However, Villeneuve delighted the *tifosi* by crowding him in second place, with Pironi riding shotgun and Prost dropping back almost straight away and retiring on the seventh lap with engine failure.

Villeneuve even squeezed ahead of Arnoux for four laps, until Rene resumed control on the 31st, while Pironi moved temporarily ahead of Gilles between laps 35 and 40. But when Arnoux's Renault also lost its engine on the 44th lap it was Villeneuve's Ferrari that was in its wake, and to Gilles this settled the matter. He would win the race. After all, back in 1979 he had honoured a similar deal when Ferrari had decided that whichever of its drivers was ahead on points at Monaco would be favoured to win the title. Gilles had duly sat right behind Jody Scheckter as they finished first and second at Monza, and such sporting self-discipline had cost him his own aspirations. Besides being the fastest driver ever seen in Formula One, Villeneuve was also a man of honour, which is why what happened over the remaining 16 laps incensed him so much.

Pironi came round him to take the lead on the 46th lap, and he held it until the 49th, when Gilles overtook him again. Then Didier led again from laps 53 to 58, when once again Gilles moved ahead in readiness for his victory, although he was a little concerned that he had been rudely chopped-off during one attempt.

If the plan was for Villeneuve to win, the seeds of an idea began to flourish that Pironi had other plans. Their cars were evenly matched, and on the final lap the Frenchman blew past Villeneuve on the high-speed run down to *Tosa*, cutting across his team-mate's bows and leaving the astonished French-Canadian nowhere else to launch a counter-attack. Pironi went on to win, leaving Villeneuve speechless with inner rage at his team-mate's stunning duplicity.

To the crowd and the television spectators it seemed like a brilliant race, with the two Ferrari drivers swapping places until Pironi finally outfumbled Villeneuve on the last lap. But Villeneuve thought otherwise, and the lap times lent weight to his views. While he had been leading, Gilles had deliberately slowed the pace, obeying pit signals to that effect, and ever mindful that Imola was always a very close call on fuel. Yet whenever Pironi was ahead their pace speeded up, endangering their chances of eking out their fuel. Once the Renaults had gone the opposition had disappeared.

Michele Alboreto, giving Tyrrell a good run in its first appearance for Candy, was third, but a long way back, and was clearly no threat. Until the last lap Villeneuve had thought that Pironi was simply playing to the gallery, risking things a little, perhaps, but apparently just giving the crowd something to keep it amused. By the time he realized that this was not the case it was too late to do anything about it.

Harvey Postlethwaite, who had produced a sanitary, honeycomb aluminium monocoque chassis for Ferrari to replace the previous year's brute, provides another suggestion as to why the two red cars might have been swapping places so often during the race: "It's a quite interesting technical note that nobody ever really knew. And that's that the reason they were overtaking each other, backwards and forwards, was not because they were actually racing, but because the control over the turbo wastegate was very, very rudimentary in those days. It was quite normal for the car to have a couple of good laps and a couple of bad laps, because the turbo pressure was very, very difficult to control. Most of the reason that they were able to pass one another so evenly was that one would go through a sort of sticky patch and sort of only be giving 4-bar of boost or 4.2, and the other would be getting a burst of 4.5, so it would have the legs of the other guy. It wasn't quite as spectacular as it appeared at the time.

"The big difference then, I think, was that the audience then were much more enthusiastic than they are now. Although we still attract big crowds to Formula One, particularly, oddly enough, in Italy, I get the feeling that they are much more jaundiced than they used to be. I mean, they were very enthusiastic then. The support that Ferrari had then – they'd just won the World Championship and they were still very much front-runners, and they hadn't been through so many of the upheavals they subsequently went through – gave you the feeling that there was much stronger and warmer support than you get today. Now, perhaps, you get the sort of football crowd, but that wasn't the case then. Maybe it's just the 'good old days' sort of thing, but I don't think it is. You got the feeling that they were just turned on by motor racing. Okay, they were very supportive of Ferrari; nowadays, at Silverstone you get the feeling that they want to see Damon Hill – Brit – rub Michael Schumacher's – German – nose in the dirt. Whereas then the support of Villeneuve in Ferrari was something; people would crawl over broken bottles to see him drive. I don't think that people go to see drivers drive now. I mean, there's that picture of Villeneuve climbing out of the car with no suspension on it, no gearbox, after that shunt... It's just an incredible image. That's what people loved. They loved him for that."

Didier was all smiles as he sprayed the champagne, but up on the rostrum Gilles' face was a stony mask, everything about his body language suggesting complete disdain for the Frenchman. It was not long before the rumours of a massive rift began filtering round the paddock. One can only imagine his feelings at that moment of defeat, for here, next to him, showering adoring *tifosi* with the champagne that he felt rightly to have been his, was the man who had stolen his win. The man who, not weeks earlier, he had asked journalists to go easy on because Didier was still suffering the after-effects of a terrifying accident in testing, when he had gone off the road at the daunting *Signes* curve at Paul Ricard at close to 180mph. The man he had helped acclimatize himself to the Ferrari camp not 12 months before.

Postlethwaite didn't get the impression that the drama was as great as it later transpired to be. "I mean, Gilles was all right. I think the whole thing was much more blown up. Villeneuve was really upset because he felt he should have been handed the race on a plate, but they were all right. The car was going reasonably well, and they were competitive, and either of them could win, sort of thing. I think it was all blown up out of all proportion, really, by the press. Two days later they were all right, really. They were okay. They weren't natural friends. Gilles was a pretty straightforward bloke, but Pironi was a very strange guy, a real oddball."

Alan Henry once told me how he had seen Hans Stuck raging at Pironi after a BMW Procar race at Hockenheim, where clearly Didier had done something to upset the tall Austrian in a big way. Like Mansell, Pironi was a driver who tended to sweat a great deal when racing, but underneath all that he was ice cool. As Stuck ranted at him, his face only an inch away, Pironi's expression barely changed and he did not flinch once, his entire manner suggesting boredom and the question "Have you finished yet?"

"He had a very strange private life," Postlethwaite recalled. "He had a real strange background. His father lived with two women, who were sisters. So his brother was his cousin... His brother raced, Jose Dolhem.

His father lived with the two women at the same time. As a result, Didier had an interesting set of morals. He was the famous one who had his wife sitting outside the Ferrari motorhome on the quay at Monaco, and he was inside with his girlfriend... It happened, that's genuine! He was a mighty strange guy, very difficult. I mean, Gilles was very easy to talk to and get close to, but Didier was a much more difficult guy to get close to. I was naturally much more friendly with Gilles than I ever was with Didier, and Didier's English wasn't that good. Mind you, neither was Gilles', come to that!"

Gilles, however, notwithstanding Postlethwaite's impression, did feel very strongly about the situation, very strongly indeed. He was literally stunned that anybody could do such a thing to him. And later that week he poured his heart out to Roebuck, who recorded it in his *Autosport* column: "When I want someone to stay behind... well, I think he stays behind. No way would he have passed me, nor would anyone else. Not on the last lap...

"Can you imagine a scene where two Ferraris, leading a race in Italy, run out of fuel on the last lap? That was the only thought in my head. So I lapped in 1-37, 1-38 for three laps, and then he passes me again, and now we're back in the 1-35s. I thought it was bloody stupid.

"Then, on lap 59, I passed him again on the approach to *Tosa*. I thought he lifted a little, but he says he had a small engine problem. Whatever it was, I got by, and even at that stage I thought he was being honest, he was obeying the original pit signal. He'd left it late, but never mind. I led that lap having slowed the pace again.

"I went into the last lap so easily you can't believe it, still very worried about the fuel. I changed up a thousand revs early. I was almost cruising down the straight towards *Tosa* because I was not expecting him to pass me again at all! And all of a sudden I saw him coming up on me. I didn't block him – if you look at the TV you will see that I never defended myself against him. And he comes inside me with the wheels almost locked, passes and wins the race. He let me by on lap 59 because he wanted to draft me at the same place on lap 60. And I was stupid enough to believe he was just being honourable.

"After the race I thought that everyone would realize what had happened, but no. Pironi says that we both had engine problems, and that there were no team orders, and what really pissed me off was that [Marco] Piccinini confirmed that to the press. My engine was perfect, and there were team orders.

"Finishing second is one thing... I would have been mad at myself for not being quick enough if he had beaten me. But finishing second because the bastard steals it... Jesus, that's why I'm mad! Everyone seems to think we had the fight of our lives, which is a joke!"

Later, Nigel told me: "When I think of that conversation that we had, two days after the race, a more conniving bloke would have weighed things up very carefully in what he said, but Gilles just poured his heart out. That was him, so open; if he felt something, he couldn't keep it bottled up."

Gilles Villeneuve never recovered from the sense of betrayal he felt that day, April 25, at Imola. And afterwards he vowed that he would not speak again with Didier Pironi. Not ever.

On May 8, a Friday, he went out to try and beat the time Pironi had set during the final minutes of first qualifying at Zolder for the Belgian Grand Prix. Past form suggested that he would better it by a reasonable margin. At 1.51pm his Ferrari somersaulted over the back of Jochen Mass' slowing March, in precisely the sort of accident he had predicted to Roebuck earlier in the year, and he was killed.

Later that year Pironi had the World Championship chalice dashed from his lips in a similar accident when he crashed into the back of Prost's Renault in the rain during final qualifying at Hockenheim. He was luckier than Gilles for his car landed at a different angle, but he nevertheless sustained horrible leg injuries that put an end to his Formula One career. He came back to motorsport after a series of unpleasant, punishing operations, to race offshore powerboats with distinction, but he was killed in an accident in the Needles Trophy race in 1987. Predictably, he had not backed off the throttle as he and his crew ran through the wash of a tanker, and at well over 100mph his boat, *Colibri 4*, had flipped and sunk.

They had never made their peace.

UNCLE KEN'S PROTEST

In what most saw as the sort of tongue-in-cheek move that only he could make, Ken Tyrrell protested the turbo cars of Ferrari, Renault and Toleman on the basis that they used turbines in their power systems, and that turbines *per se* were not allowed under the rules.

Some observers believed that this was not just Tyrrell being awkward, but shrewdly covering his back, making a small show of solidarity with the FOCA ranks he had been obliged to break by commercial necessity. Certainly, these cannot have been easy days for the man who won World Championships with Jackie Stewart in 1969, 1971 and 1973, and many sympathized with his precarious and ticklish position.

The stewards of the meeting, flustered at first, breathed a sigh of relief when they realized they could fall back on use of the word turbine to mean engines such as the gas turbine raced by Lotus in 1971 and 1972. Moreover, they pointed out with growing confidence, the regulations did allow for piston engines to be fitted with superchargers, and the turbines to which Tyrrell referred were merely the impellers (turbines) within the turbo compressors that the cars were entitled to use. They then made the rather uneasy distinction that the turbo engines gained their power by movement of rods and pistons, and not by the explosion of gas, which took a bit of believing since ignition and expansion of fuel in the cylinders is, of course, an intrinsic part of the functioning of an Otto-cycle engine.

The protest was thrown out, and two years later Tyrrell suddenly fell foul of authority for allegedly using water as ballast and illegal fuel additives, as a consequence of which all of his 1984 results were effectively expunged from the record books. Some interpreted this as Bernie Ecclestone getting his own back for Tyrrell's FOCA defection that weekend at Imola.

7
When Patrick drove for Gilles

"I swear it wasn't me driving that car that day. It felt as if Gilles was there with me..." – Patrick Tambay

Few Grand Prix victories can ever have been quite so emotional as that achieved by Patrick Tambay and Ferrari at Imola on May 1, 1983. It was one of those magical affairs when the crowd gets exactly what it wants, when the victor himself is universally popular, and when everything appears guided by an unseen hand as events unravel. One by one, Patrick Tambay's rivals wilted, making mistakes of their own and leaving him clear to drive home to a delirious reception in car 27 – the car which bore the number made legendary by the *tifosi*'s hero Gilles Villeneuve – and the car which they firmly believed should have won the previous year's race. Villeneuve, of course, was gone, killed in qualifying for the Belgian Grand Prix almost a year earlier. But for the *tifosi* – and for Patrick – his spirit lived on that day.

"Winning that race was very emotional for me," Tambay would relate years later. "That race was just so extraordinary for me. In Germany in 1982 I had felt very keenly the responsibility that rested on my shoulders when I took over the seat left by Gilles, but Imola was much, much more."

Ferrari was always in with a chance this year, which would be the first in which a turbocharged car would take a driver to the World Championship now that ground effects had been seriously limited by the introduction of flat-bottom chassis. Gone, for the Prancing Horse, were the years when the behaviour of its cars had emanated the black horse motif that Enzo Ferrari had 'borrowed' from the World War One flying ace Francesco Baracca and mounted on the yellow background of Modena. Instead, Harvey Postlethwaite's pen had produced the carbon-fibre 126C2/B, an elegant and efficient car which Rene Arnoux used to great effect to dominate practice as he edged out Nelson Piquet's fleet Brabham-BMW in both sessions. In the end the little Frenchman took pole position with a lap of 1m 33.238s to Piquet's 1m 33.964s. By a twist of fate, that in its turn just beat Tambay's best by three-thousandths of a second and left Patrick to occupy third place on the grid. That would be crucial to the unfolding story.

"My car had given me plenty of trouble," said Patrick, who had battled with loss of turbo boost on his engine on Friday, and had then blown a piston when he tried running higher pressure. He also admitted that whereas Arnoux had opted for Goodyear's softest E-compound tyres, he had been a mite more cautious in choosing Ds. "By coincidence, all of this meant that I lined up in the same position that Gilles had had in the previous year's race when Didier Pironi had won. Poor Gilles, he never, ever got over that. He felt so cheated!"

Raceday dawned to brilliant sunshine, but as an estimated 100,000 *tifosi* flocked into the circuit in the confident expectation that one or other of the Ferraris was going to win, Tambay had an emotional experience that he kept to himself and those closest to him at the time.

"Right ahead of me on the grid was a Canadian Maple Leaf that the *tifosi* had painted on the track where Gilles had lined his car up. I felt very, very emotional thinking about him just before the start. I was sitting in my car on the grid with 20 minutes to go, and I just broke down, you know...

"I was just sitting there, crying my eyes out. I was completely broken up. My mechanics, my friends who came to the car to wish me luck, just walked away. They were embarrassed for me, and didn't know what to do or what to say. There was nothing any of them could have said or done.

"I felt better when the race started, and I ran second in the early stages to my team-mate Arnoux, who had started from the pole position. Then Riccardo Patrese passed me in the second Brabham. I took over the lead when Riccardo was delayed during his stop for tyres."

Piquet had stalled his Brabham at the start, leaving Patrese to take up the cudgels for Bernie's team. Arnoux and Tambay ran first and second for the first two laps before Patrese dived into second place, which became first by the sixth lap as he eased ahead of Rene going through *Rivazza*. Up until his disastrous pit stop on lap 34, Riccardo looked as if he had the race well sewn up as he controlled a 27-second lead, but then it all began to go wrong.

Herbie Blash recalled that incident with a grimace. "What a prick! Riccardo overshot the pit. He had the race in his pocket, and he came in too fast and just went straight by where he should have stopped!" As a mechanic tried to make an air hammer reach the white and blue car, its pneumatic hose popped off. Riccardo didn't help things again by forgetting to keep the brakes on during the wheel change.

After this tragi-comedy of errors as his car was dragged back and serviced, he surged back into what was by then a very different race, having been at a standstill for 23.3 seconds. Tambay had gone into the lead and had built up a 10.6-second cushion. Bit by bit Riccardo got his head down and began to close the gap, aided by a misfire which afflicted the Ferrari through the long run of *Tamburello*. By lap 47 the gap was less than five seconds, and by lap 52 it was down to one and a half and the crowd was on tenterhooks. Surely Ferrari wasn't going to lose so close to the end!

On the 55th lap the groans of dismay of the *tifosi* were audible as the Brabham swept ahead on the run down to *Tosa*. Insouciantly, Riccardo exited the hairpin with a sliver of oversteer, as if celebrating his imminent triumph. But then, incredibly, only two corners later he ran wide going through *Acque Minerali*.

Since the early laps, sections of the track surface had shown signs of breaking up in the torrid heat and the passage of the more powerful cars, and even a star with the experience of Niki Lauda had been caught out when he shunted his McLaren on the 12th lap. Earlier, too, Johnny Cecotto had spun his Theodore at *Acque Minerali*. Now, in a moment, the 'marbles' had grasped at the Brabham and dragged it relentlessly to the left of the track in a deadly understeering slide that took it over the grass before it speared helplessly into the tyre wall. It was one of the most catastrophic mistakes of recent times, a lead squandered, a race lost.

Tambay, still pushing in the Ferrari, swept back ahead as the crestfallen Riccardo climbed from the wreckage. It was little consolation to him that Arnoux also had a brief spin there that same lap on his way to third place behind Tambay and Prost's Renault, which had lost fourth gear and some of its power, and had gained unwanted understeer. Further back, determined performances from Rosberg, Watson and Surer went largely unnoticed.

There had been other incidents, too. Cheever and Jarier squared up to one another after a coming-together during the morning warm-up, while Roberto Guerrero and Danny Sullivan never saw eye-to-eye on blame for the incident on lap three in which the American inadvertently pitched the Colombian into the tyres at *Villeneuve*. Later still, Danny lost it himself and hit Derek Warwick's abandoned Toleman at *Rivazza*. But none of these could be compared with Riccardo's misfortune. The crowd was delirious with joy, and nobody would have guessed that a local boy had just lost the lead of his national race.

"It just went to show that Ferrari is more important than an Italian driver," Brabham team owner Bernie Ecclestone observed, as the crowd catcalled Patrese on his long, embarrassing and depressing trudge back to the pits. "I didn't say anything to him when he walked back in. What are you going to say? He's fallen off the road... There's no point in pointing anything out to somebody that's the obvious. He already knew what he'd done wrong. He didn't need me to tell him, did he? I mean, when you ruck somebody you give them the chance; better to let them stew on their own, isn't it?"

Riccardo knew precisely what he'd done, alright, and he had plenty of time to let it sink in as his generous countrymen booed and jeered him and cheered on their beloved Ferrari and the Frenchman at its wheel.

Imola 1983 was a monkey which would sit on Patrese's back for years. "For a loss of concentration, I lose the race," he sighed, still regretful, seven years later. "Because, you know, the trouble is that I thought I had won. Yes, I think that was it. When I got back into the lead after that pit stop I just relaxed for a moment, and because there were all those marbles where the track was breaking up, I just went 10 centimetres too wide and the car went off, and I lost the Grand Prix because of that. From that moment on I always had a weight in my stomach because I could not win Imola..."

Patrick, conversely, carried a different kind of weight because he could win.

"I drove that race in a dream," he admitted. "I don't know if you believe in metaphysics or whatever, but I swear it wasn't me driving that car that day. It felt as if Gilles was there with me, as if he was doing the work. All round the track there were banners saying things like 'Gilles and Patrick – two hearts, one number!', but I knew they were for him, not me. I was just driving his car, and after what had happened the previous year I desperately wanted to win this one."

The Ferrari was beautiful on that day of days, apart from that one desperately worrying thing as it kept stuttering through *Tamburello*, where each lap Patrick suffered the terrors of uncertainty that he would finish.

"In the closing stages, after Patrese had crashed and I was leading again, it actually kept cutting out as I went through there, and my heart was in my mouth. I was thinking, 'Please don't let it stop now!', and I was so relieved that it kept going. But then it stopped altogether, out of fuel, on the slowing-down lap. The crowd just went crazy!" Indeed, Patrick was pulled bodily from his stranded car by the excited and none-too-gentle *tifosi*, and carried aloft in triumph until an official car arrived to escort him safely back to the podium.

"Imola has so much atmosphere, doesn't it?" says Blash. "The one thing about Imola that always springs to my mind is that it was a Villeneuve circuit, even though he never won there. If you go around the back, even today, you will always see the photos of Gilles – and even though Senna is taking over, there are not many circuits that have this kind of eerie feeling about them. Pictures of Gilles in his coffin, that sort of thing... But it wasn't macabre. They loved him."

This was one of the most emotional triumphs of the Eighties as the Ferrari sped beneath the chequered flag and the *tifosi* erupted into an orgasm of delight. By the time he had been brought back to the safety of the victory rostrum Patrick Tambay was himself again, and there, with a quiet dedication, he gave the win to Gilles, "To the memory of the car number 27 which didn't win last year."

Patrick always was a man of extraordinary class.

MANSELL'S LUCKY ESCAPE

Nigel Mansell had some shunts during his career, but the accident that befell him on the 57th lap of the 1983 San Marino Grand Prix must rate as one of the most frightening.

Trapped in the uncompetitive Cosworth-powered Lotus 92B, the Englishman had simply got on with the job with his customary determination at a time in his career when few really saw the latent talent that would subsequently emerge in better machinery. Starting 15th, he had worked his way up as high as 10th before dropping steadily back, and he was running near the tail of the field in the closing stages when the elaborate four-tier rear wing simply sheared off as he sped down through *Villeneuve* at maximum speed. The Lotus snapped violently out of control and spun three times through 360 degrees before ending up tail-first in the barriers. A white-faced Mansell limped away from what could have been a very serious accident.

He was never Peter Warr's favourite driver. Indeed, it was the former Lotus manager who once coined the memorable phrase: "Nigel Mansell won't be World Champion as long as he's got a hole in his arse!"

But that day, as Mansell fought doggedly on until his great drama, Warr's favoured man, Elio de Angelis, acquitted himself poorly. Disappointed that he had had to switch to the team's spare car after his own 93T had blown a turbo just before the grid parade lap, he tugged round with no heart in what he was doing before finally pulling into the pits to quit after 44 unimpressive laps. Even Warr was moved to comment afterwards, through tightly clenched teeth: "We pay our drivers to race, and sometimes Elio needs to be reminded of that." At least he never had any trouble with Mansell on that score.

8
Lessons for the learning

"It was one of the things that even Ayrton would admit, that he did learn a lot from Alain when he first started driving for us at McLaren. But in 1984 and 1985 it was very hard for him. He just wanted to be the lion..."
– Jo Ramirez

The face of Formula One had changed several times in the early Eighties, but as things had settled down at the end of 1983, when the flat-bottomed chassis regulations had been in effect for a season, further rule amendments were scheduled and these opened up another new era. In 1983, teams had been allowed to fit fuel tanks of up to 250 litres and could make as many refuelling stops as they liked; for 1984 that figure was cut by 30 litres, and at the 11th hour refuelling was banned altogether on safety grounds. By 1986, the 220-litre allowance had further been savaged, this time to only 195 litres, and over this three-year period massive strides were made in the development of computer controls in engine management systems, for besides employing frugal drivers, herein lay the real key to speed with economy, and ultimately victory.

Grand Prix racing thus entered an era where that economy – and for much of the time fuel conservation – were of paramount importance. The racing itself suffered a great deal, as onboard computer read-outs in front of the drivers would warn them if they had dug themselves into fuel debt, and they would then have to back off until the figures came right again.

Sometimes, of course, no amount of back-pedalling could restore that critical balance, and nowhere was this problem more pronounced than at Imola, the hardest circuit on fuel in the calendar, where races frequently ended with otherwise healthy cars stranded by the roadside for the want of a few more litres of juice, and highly frustrated drivers clambering angrily from their cockpits.

In the three Imola races of the mid-decade, Alain Prost would show time and again that brilliant ability both to pace himself and to conserve his car and its systems while running a race underwritten with cunning;

but for the vagaries of fortune, he would have won on all three occasions. This was the era when the Frenchman was demonstrating, with the backing of a top team, not only how to put race wins together consistently, but eventually how to win World Championships, too, after his disappointing near-miss with Renault in 1983. Moreover, for his first two years with McLaren he was doing so while coping with one of the smartest team-mates in the business: Niki Lauda. Then in 1986, following Niki's second retirement from the sport in six years (and this time he really meant it), Prost's partner was to be one of the fastest drivers around: Keke Rosberg.

This was also the period when a brilliant young Brazilian star called Ayrton Senna was learning, first of all how to go about Formula One racing, and then, once he had defected from Toleman to Lotus, how to win races.

By 1984, all of the serious contenders had turbocharged engines, only Ken Tyrrell proving capable of any show of force on occasion with cars still powered by the old faithful normally aspirated Cosworth Ford DFY. And of all the teams, McLaren was proving the most consistently adept at coping with the new rules whilst simultaneously learning how to win consistently in F1 under the new management of Ron Dennis and John Barnard, who had effectively taken over from Teddy Mayer in 1981 at Marlboro's behest.

They won the first two races of the 1984 season (the first with Prost and the second with Lauda), but then they learned the hard way how not to win the Belgian Grand Prix in Zolder, where a change of fuel caused lots of TAG Porsche combustion headaches. Instead, Michele Alboreto had taken the victory for Ferrari, and as the race in Belgium immediately preceded the San Marino Grand Prix, the Italian fans were all set for a repeat performance by Ferrari on home ground.

However, revealing a startling grasp of how to do the job thoroughly, Ron Dennis had sent his team back to Woking during the week between the two races to try to sort out the problems with the mismatch between the revised fuel and the Bosch management chips. Then came the rush back to Imola, where, despite some minor engine and brake problems, Prost wound up second on the grid after Nelson Piquet just managed to pip his lap time of 1m 28.628s to snaffle the pole with minutes of the session remaining. With Keke Rosberg's Williams-Honda and Derek Warwick's Renault on the second row ahead of Lauda's McLaren-TAG and Arnoux's Ferrari, a strong contest was envisaged, but Prost would see to it that there was no contest at all.

In contrast to practice, which had been run in uncharacteristically inclement weather, things brightened a little on race day in time for Prost to snatch the lead right from the start. As Rosberg's Williams baulked on the line, Lauda, right behind, also had gear selection problems, and the two of them got away late. Such was Prost's complete superiority that afternoon that he was able to indulge himself with a spin at the first *Rivazza* on his 23rd lap, then gather things up, and later make a pit stop for four fresh Michelins, without looking even remotely like losing his lead. As for the pirouette, the Frenchman initially thought he had simply let himself get caught out under braking, but it would transpire later that a faulty master-cylinder had been the cause of this, his only problem.

In his wake his rivals had a troubled afternoon. Piquet ran second before being overtaken by Warwick, who even then was trying to obey the dictates of his computer to save fuel. Nelson repassed Derek on lap 27 in a repeat of their Formula Three battles of old, but then succumbed to a blown turbo. Lauda, meanwhile, had staged a brilliant recovery, driving as if he was still with BRM and trying to make a name for himself in the early Seventies, but after 15 laps, just as he had been shaping up for a rare fight with Warwick, his McLaren had broken its engine.

Rosberg, too, was an early retirement with electrical failure, as was Alboreto, who had had a miserable time in qualifying with the second Ferrari before succumbing to a loss of turbo boost, caused by a loose exhaust pipe. With 20 laps to go, when Warwick was slowed by a baulky gear shift and the eventual loss of fourth gear, Arnoux had come through to take second place, well behind the leading McLaren. Elio de Angelis, too, had pushed ahead of Warwick, only to run out of fuel on the last lap. Worried about suffering the same fate, Warwick had allowed Prost to lap him; had he been unlapped he could have passed the Lotus to reclaim third and a podium finish, but there was no way of getting the information across to him. Pit-to-car radios were still some way off...

As a taster of what was to come in subsequent years, a brilliant charge from the back of the field to third place by Andrea de Cesaris proved to have been at the expense of his fuel ration, and the Italian's Ligier-Renault ground to a halt with two laps left. Eddie Cheever, too, ran dry after a similar effort, parking his Alfa Romeo with zero propellant. Already one lesson was crystal clear: speed was no good at all if it came at the expense of fuel...

This was never more apparent than in the 1985 race, which brought another typical Prost performance which, for once, did not provide the fruits of success that it merited. Senna was now in a car worthy of his talents, and he took his Lotus 95T to pole position in 1m 27.327s, half a second quicker than team-mate de Angelis, who was third. As history would reveal, that was probably a pretty fair indication of their respective abilities. Between them sat Rosberg's Honda-powered Williams FW10, with Alboreto's Ferrari and Thierry Boutsen's Arrows-BMW next up. This time Prost was only sixth on the grid, ahead of Mansell's Williams and Lauda's McLaren, but he was shrewd enough to know that at Imola, under the new rules, a front-row grid position was nothing like as important as a smart brain and the right balance of speed versus restraint during the race.

From the trackside this seemed like a splendid race as de Angelis pushed Senna very hard in the opening laps in a Lotus 1-2, but this, remember, was the era when all was not always what it seemed. "As a team, we enjoyed that era of fuel economy Formula One," said Ron Dennis. "We were part of it, it was quite good. You know, dialling things in and watching through telemetry all the fuel usage and everything. How you could influence it. We were far better equipped to control the fuel settings than the drivers, so we would instruct them to change the fuel setting and vary the revs, and we could monitor the influence on fuel consumption. Of course, we did that in practice as well, but in the race you could actually calculate at a given setting what you needed to get through."

However, though it was undoubtedly a fascinating exercise for those engineers and personnel who were in the privileged position of knowing precisely what was going on, and why, for the spectators this era of Formula One racing was a bust.

Lauda spun early on when his onboard computer played up, throwing up a warning light at him at the chicane and then suddenly cutting-out the engine, which left the Austrian with a nerve-straining afternoon ahead of him. Prost, meanwhile, had his hands full trying to pass Alboreto who, being a Ferrari driver racing at Imola, was not about to give third place away without the sort of black fight he could produce when he felt backed into a corner. To prove his point to Prost, he elbowed him on to the dirt on the climb out of *Tosa* on lap eight, and Alain decided that discretion was the better part of valour, at least for the time being. At this time de Angelis was also in a spot of trouble with fading rear brakes, dropping behind Michele on lap 11 and behind Prost a lap later. At the same time, Piquet was pushing forward in his Pirelli-shod Brabham, rising to sixth ahead of Rosberg and leaving Mansell to fend off Boutsen and Cheever as the Briton drove with one eye on his fuel gauge.

Senna was clearly on a high after scoring his first Grand Prix victory in the wet in Portugal, which was the previous race, and he looked well set to repeat that success on a dry track. But on lap 19 he put a wheel in the dirt at *Piratella* as Alboreto briefly thrust the Ferrari at him. He recovered his momentum rapidly, and then the Italian threat disappeared as Prost pulled one of his brilliant overtaking moves on Michele to flash by the Ferrari round the outside on the run down to *Rivazza*. Shortly after that the red car's engine began to run roughly, and though Michele returned to set fastest lap after a pit stop to rectify the problem, he retired with battery failure.

Prost was now clear to chase after Senna, but the Brazilian did not seem in the least bit intimidated by the presence of the man who had missed winning the previous year's World Championship by the narrowest ever margin of half a point. It was a foretaste of what we would become used to in a few years' time. The McLaren was quicker on the run through *Tamburello* and down to *Tosa*, but Senna used some unusual lines and repeatedly rebuffed Prost's advances. It was gripping stuff, but was it for real?

On the 34th lap Senna came up to pass Patrick Tambay's Renault before *Piratella*, and in a move that would become so familiar he simply scythed past the Frenchman without the slightest hesitation, leaving Prost to struggle momentarily behind the yellow car. It was classic Senna.

Prost kept up the pressure until the 38th lap, then obeyed the dictates of his dashboard readout and eased back to conserve fuel. This, too, was classic stuff, the sort of self-discipline that only the Frenchman seemed able to master. Further back, Lauda's push had abated as he began losing gears; fifth went away, and then he had to start holding fourth in engagement. That let Stefan Johansson, recently promoted from Tyrrell to the Ferrari squad, up into fourth place behind de Angelis. The Swede was driving flat-out, to the rapturous delight of the *tifosi*.

By lap 54, Stefan was ahead of Prost and running second as he began to attack Senna's 10-second lead. The crowd was on its feet at the prospect of a Ferrari winning, but again appearances were deceptive, as they were about to discover. Senna had begun to realize that his fuel situation was marginal, but he had worked it out too late. At the beginning of the season the practice of freezing fuel had been banned. By chilling it, teams had been able to cram a little more into their tanks (at least until the car's temperature warmed it and it began to evaporate from the breather), but now those who were really marginal were about to face the music. As Senna crossed the line to lead into the 57th lap his Renault V6 stuttered, caught again, and then stuttered on the run to *Tosa*, where he cruised to a halt. He was out of juice, and his initial speed fell into perspective.

In only his second race for Ferrari, Stefan Johansson was now leading, but the ecstasy only lasted until *Acque Minerali*, where his rags-to-riches story went the same way as his final dregs of Agip. Here was another who had gone too fast, too soon, and for too long.

"I turned down the boost from half-distance onwards and was convinced I had sufficient fuel," said the crestfallen Swede. "I was driving balls-out the whole way, and I reckon I could have lapped in the 1m 31s all day if I had to..."

"Stefan was about to be a hero, and then he ran out round the back," reflected Harvey Postlethwaite with a groan some years later, adding at the recollection: "Oh, Jesus, don't... Those fuel regulations were bloody stupid. Imola was always a bloody difficult race to finish for fuel.

Basically, you'd design the fuel tank for Imola, in the autumn, when you were drawing the car, and by the time you got to Imola for the race the engine people would have found a few more horsepower, using a bit more fuel, and you had a problem. Imola and Canada were the two nasty ones on fuel because of all the acceleration and braking."

So Prost ran out the winner after a beautifully judged race, even though he, too, ran out of fuel, but only on the slowing-down lap, while de Angelis survived wear in his rear brake pads that was so excessive that the piston had popped out of one of the calipers. He finished second, ahead of Boutsen's well-driven Arrows. The Belgian, too, was in fuel trouble, and deliberately allowed his car to stammer to the line but didn't cross it until Prost had finished his final lap, knowing that he did not have enough aboard to do another 100 yards, let alone another lap. Further back, Tambay was unaware that, had he speeded up, he would have pipped the Arrows for the last podium spot.

Lauda soldiered on to fifth place ahead of Mansell, who had also driven with iron control and obeyed what his fuel readout told him throughout. At that stage of his career he needed finishes more than he needed heroics. Johansson was classified seventh and Senna eighth, and when the Lotus lads went to collect their car later they discovered that one of its rear tyres had a slow puncture. While they were doing that, Peter Warr was discovering that his team had won the race after all...

As FISA carried out its routine weight check on the leading cars, Prost's McLaren continuously failed to make the minimum figure of 540kg. In the end there was nothing to do but disqualify it for being underweight. So now de Angelis had won one of the last victories for Lotus, while Boutsen was elevated to second place, the closest Arrows would ever get to a win.

"Alain did a fantastic job to keep the car going to the finish, and unfortunately it was 0.8 of a kilogramme light at the end," McLaren's Jo Ramirez remembers. "It was so marginal that they had to weigh the car several times, and I have to say that FISA was very fair about it.

"Alain had run out of fuel on the slowing-down lap, and the difference we were under was so little... If he would have got into the marbles off the circuit and collected some stones on the tyres, he would probably have just made that 0.8! It was just very unfortunate. I can't remember what the computer in the car was telling us, but we couldn't always trust what it was saying.

"I tell you, if we would have lost the Championship for nine points at the end of the year, I don't think I would ever have been able to look Alain in his face, for having lost him the Championship... He took it very bravely. It was one of the things I always admired him for. He said, 'Well, I won a lot of races by being on the weight limit, and I lost this by being a little under it.' He took it very well. And fortunately we still won the

Championship without those points..." Though he was gracious in defeat, Prost would later admit that losing that race hurt more than losing the 1984 World Championship by that half-point to Lauda.

Memory can play funny tricks. Ron Dennis, the man who once said: "We make history, you just write about it," to the assembled press corps, does not recall Prost running out of fuel. "No, Alain didn't run out on the slowing-down lap," he averred. "He actually completed it. The fuel we used on that lap would have been enough to keep the car within the weight limit. In fact, I think it was a little less than 0.8 of a kilo light. It was fluctuating every time we weighed it, but the problem was that we couldn't get it to go over the weight limit. If he'd picked up dirt on the tyres... It's something that can be done and has been done, but I think that the frustration is not that result; you make mistakes, and we made one, and we paid the price for it and lost that race. Such is life."

The situation clearly rankles Dennis even today, however. "What's particularly frustrating is not so much that result, but the amount of times that things have happened on other people's cars," he continued. "They to me are greater in their inconsistency as regards to the rule interpretation, and the penalty hasn't been so severe. My biggest frustration has been, and always will be, inconsistent application of the regulations.

"Alain was philosophical. I think in 1985 he and Ayrton were both still going up their learning curves, but then again, aren't we all? If nothing else, 1985 was an interesting tactical race."

A litre of fuel weighs around 3kg, which indicates just how tight was Prost's margin of penalty. That evening Nigel Roebuck left the circuit in company with Dennis and Ramirez. "Jo was just distraught, while Ron was pretty serious, too," he recalled. "And Ron said to Jo: 'We'd better make bloody sure that we are more than nine points ahead at the end of the Championship...' I was very aware of the affection and depth of feeling for Alain in the team at that time."

The result made something of a mockery of Formula One, but Steve Nichols, who at that time was race engineering at McLaren, put a similar strong case for the regulations as Dennis had, while providing an insight into Prost's successful tactics:

"I thought it was a very interesting formula. There was all this talk all the time of taxi drivers and economy runs, and things like that, and perhaps it wasn't brilliant for the spectators, but from where we stand they all look the same anyway. They just flash past in a straight line. It was a very interesting technical exercise and it was all about efficiency, and so forth, and it was really interesting on the circuit. It was so much more of a chess game for the drivers.

"So many times Prost would drive himself into fuel debt, so to speak, to break the back of the competition, and then spend the rest of the race dragging it back slowly but surely. So many times in those seasons I thought: 'That's it, we're stalled. We're history. We can never make it back from this.' But Prost would drag it back little by little and finish the race.

"As an example, I remember Montreal in 1988, when we were being pressured by Boutsen in a normally aspirated Benetton, and I'm quite sure with the boost levels that we had to run there that we had less horsepower than the normally aspirated cars: 575bhp or something. Like Imola, we were marginal on fuel, but when Boutsen kept on pushing, Prost would keep on pushing further and further into fuel debt, and then finally Boutsen would give up a little and Alain would get it back. It was really a balancing act. He was really the best at that."

A balancing act honed at tracks such as Imola, with its heavy demands on economy in those middle-Eighties years.

"It might have been a little boring for the spectators," Nichols concedes, "but for us, watching the numbers on the screen, it was really sort of fascinating all the time! Those were interesting times. They were brilliant races."

At that time Tim Wright was Prost's race engineer, and he provides an illuminating reason as to why the McLaren failed the weight check.

"At that time we weren't consciously ballasting the car, it had never been a problem. But at that particular race he ran out of fuel and he didn't actually do a slow-down lap. On the last lap he was weaving the car because he was having a fuel pick-up problem, and I'm sure he just coasted across the line. He got across it and stopped not far beyond. I remember that Boutsen was third and he purposely crept across behind Alain so that he didn't have to do another lap.

"The other thing was not only that Alain had run out of fuel, but also that he had used an awful lot of water and engine oil. The car was something like seven kilos lighter than it normally would have been. It wasn't an unusual problem, because those TAG-Porsche engines did use a lot of water. But because of all those fluid losses he was under the weight limit by just under a kilo. It was very close."

He, too, remembers that Prost took the blow with good grace. "Alain was a bit disbelieving at first about what had happened, but when it became clear why the car was under weight he was quite good about it. To lose all those fluids was fairly rare, especially as he hadn't had too much indication about it.

"It's definitely true that Alain was the master of that period of Formula One, with his uncanny ability to pace himself. I think that he learned quite a lot of that from 1984, from Niki, with his race strategy. And likewise I think Senna subsequently learned quite a lot of that from him."

In Formula One, wheels often turn full-circle.

"There were quite a few times in '85 when he quite obviously wasn't the quickest, or the car wasn't the quickest around," Wright continued, "but just the way he did his race strategy, he always came out on top."

Prost faced even tougher opposition in 1986, with Keke Rosberg as his team-mate, Piquet joining Mansell at Williams in well-sorted Honda-powered FW11s, Senna spearheading the Lotus-Renault challenge again in the fine-handing 98T, Alboreto and Johansson paired again at Ferrari, and Toleman emerging as a new threat, but now in the guise of Benetton and powered by the same BMW four-cylinder turbo as Brabham had used in 1985. The drivers here were the taciturn Italian Teo Fabi, and an upcoming new star from Austria called Gerhard Berger, who would feature strongly and dramatically in the story of Imola.

Further down the grid, 1983 winner Patrick Tambay was driving a Beatrice Lola fitted with a Brian Hart turbo engine while Alan Jones, his team-mate in this grandiose but short-lived operation, prepared to debut its replacement, Ford's new V6 turbo. Hart's engine had helped Toleman get on its feet at Imola back in 1981, but this was scheduled to be his last race as a Formula One engine manufacturer – as opposed to an engine builder – until 1993, when he introduced his impressive V10 with the Jordan team.

True to form, Senna annexed pole position in the Lotus with a lap in 1m 25.050s, half a second faster than Piquet. Mansell and Prost shared row two, Alboreto and Rosberg row three. Johansson was seventh, sharing with Rene Arnoux, the former Ferrari star whose mercurial career had hit hard times at Ligier, and the Benettons were on the fifth row. The race would be harder still now that the teams were limited to just 195 litres of fuel per car, although there was a glimmer of hope for some when raceday dawned damp after overnight rain. It was still damp in the morning warm-up, and then there was a brief shower just before the grid formed.

The rain had stopped by the time the race got under way and Piquet snatched an early lead after passing Senna just before *Tosa*. It was not long before the fortunes of the race were established. Mansell retired after only eight laps when his engine blew after he had experienced electrical problems; then, after fading early on, Senna retired in the pits on the 11th lap with a problem with a suspension upright, which had led to rear wheel bearing failure. That left Piquet leading Rosberg, who had repassed Prost on the 13th lap and now had his French team-mate quite happily sitting economically in his slipstream.

Then Piquet realized he had run into the red on fuel, and as he backed off the McLarens closed in on him, with Alboreto 10 seconds further back and running just ahead of the Benetton duo, who had dispensed with Johansson when Stefan ran into brake trouble.

Piquet was further delayed with a slow pit stop, and while Prost was serviced quickly, Rosberg's call was also a disaster as the Finn took his foot off the brake pedal just before the left-rear wheel nut had been fully tightened, the result of a misunderstanding over Ron Dennis' signal. This meant that Prost was now leading from Rosberg, with Piquet obeying his computer read-out and conserving fuel in third place. It was not exactly racing in the grand manner.

Further back, Arnoux was into a drive that recalled his best days, dragging the Ligier into sight of Alboreto, while Patrese was also running strongly on a set of hard-compound Pirellis, and had the awkward 'lay-down' Brabham BT55 up into sixth place by the 34th lap.

Steadily, Prost eased away from Rosberg, taking as much out of his McLaren's brakes and transmission as he dared, but trying to spare the engine and the fuel all the time. But if the racing was quite muted at the front, the crowd was being entertained by Johansson's vigorous attempts to keep Berger behind as both men struggled with car problems. Stefan was having to pump his Ferrari's brakes as the pedal travel got longer and longer, while Gerhard had been taking it easy initially as his clutch had failed and he was having to shift gear without it.

But now the Austrian was flying, and as Martin Brundle's 10th-placed Tyrrell came up to pass Piercarlo Ghinzani's Osella, Gerhard grabbed the chance to box Johansson in, only to himself be pinned behind Brundle by the Swede. The issue was settled as the Benetton pushed by under braking for the *Rivazza*. It was the 54th lap and Gerhard was now sixth, but Fate was about to intervene on his behalf.

Three laps later, Alboreto's tenancy of fourth place came to an end with turbocharger failure, elevating Patrese to fourth and Berger to fifth. And then came yet another of those Imola *denouements* as the truth finally emerged about respective fuel consumptions. Piquet had saved sufficient to have one last stab at Rosberg's second place, but Keke had also been eyeing the gauge carefully and had calculated that he, too, had enough for the sprint to the line. The only problem was that his readout had been short-changing him, as he discovered to his chagrin as the McLaren stuttered impotently to a halt on its 59th lap. A lap down, Patrese became the beneficiary, but no sooner had he got used to the idea of passing Rosberg's stricken car for third place than he suffered a similar problem before he reached it.

Thus, in a remarkable six-lap period, Berger had risen from seventh to third after passing only Johansson, who rose with him to inherit fourth. Rosberg was classified fifth, with Patrese sixth, cursing his dreadful Imola fortune.

This left Prost to cruise round his last lap to take the chequered flag for the third time in three years – but then suddenly his TAG-Porsche V6 was coughing, too, as he came down out of the second *Rivazza*. Weaving desperately from side to side, the World Champion just managed to slurp

The Seventies brought back the international set. In 1970 Clay Regazzoni and Emerson Fittipaldi (running second and third here, above) were the F2 heat winners in the former's European Championship season, racing on an Imola that rather surprisingly had a good run-off area at *Tosa*, but an increasingly atypical lack of safety barriers. Six years later (below), Jean-Pierre Jarier and Jody Scheckter in their Alpine Renault sportscars battled with Jacky Ickx's ultimately victorious Martini Porsche.

Forza Il Leone! A tremendous favourite with the *tifosi*, especially when driving their beloved Ferraris, Nigel Mansell drove a commendably brave race in 1989 (above) when he elected to carry on even though the precise causes of team-mate Gerhard Berger's fiery meeting with the *Tamburello* wall had yet to be identified. That spectacular race also marked the first real outward manifestation of the simmering aggravation between Senna and Prost (below), which Ron Dennis had hitherto successfully managed to keep under a measure of control.

Have perch, will view. When it comes to spectating at motor races for minimum financial outlay, the *tifosi* have some remarkably inventive ideas, as this shot taken behind the outer wall near Rivazza (above) indicates . . . For Riccardo Patrese (below), 1990 saw the laying of a ghost when, seven years after crashing within sight of victory on home ground, he finally enjoyed his day of days.

For Patrick Tambay (above), always a sensitive character, the 1983 race was an emotional rollercoaster as he won 'for Gilles', driving Ferrari no 27, but the red cars brought only crushing disappointment for newly-signed Stefan Johansson (below) two years later. Typifying the knife-edge nature of the fuel economy years, the Swede had victory plucked from his grasp within sight of the flag, after using too much of his precious propellant.

During the mid-Eighties era when a delicate touch and the ability to control one's basic racing instincts were paramount, Alain Prost (above) stood in a class entirely on his own, and but for a McLaren miscalculation would have won the hat-trick in 1984-86. Meanwhile, the first reminder of the dangers of *Tamburello* was visited upon Piquet (conferring here in the pits with Williams technical director Patrick Head) when he crashed heavily there in practice for the 1987 race.

A Championship Grand Prix at last! In the one-off Italian Grand Prix in 1980, that year's World Champion Alan Jones takes his Williams into *Tosa* well ahead of Rene Arnoux's Renault and Nelson Piquet's Brabham (above), but the main talking point was the massive accident from which Gilles Villeneuve escaped (below) at the corner which ever afterwards bore his name.

Rain marred the inaugural San Marino Grand Prix in 1981, but that didn't deter Piquet, whose Brabham was in a class of its own after all the political wrangling that had sullied qualifying. Here (above) the Brazilian slips through traffic comprising John Watson's McLaren, Jacques Laffite's Ligier and team-mate Hector Rebaque. One year later Villeneuve's expression on the victory rostrum says everything (below) as the celebrations of his partner Didier Pironi and third placed Michele Alboreto leave him completely cold.

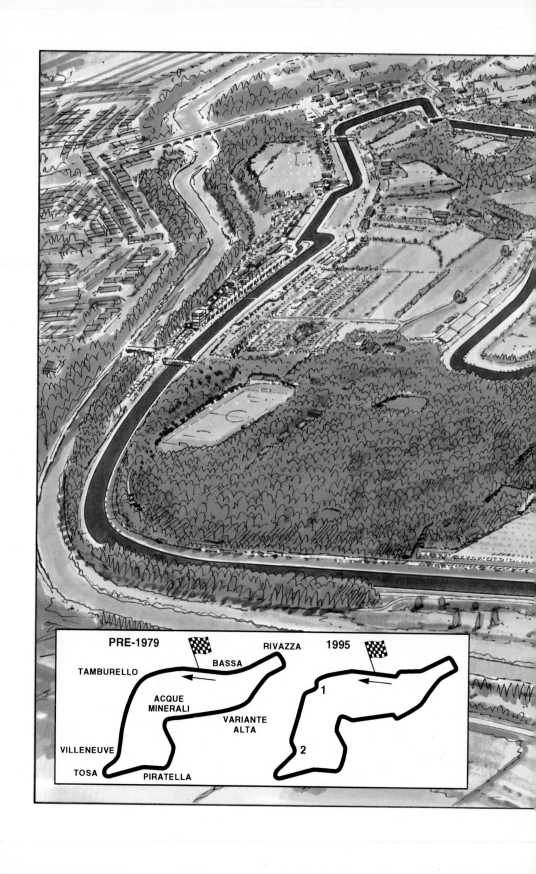

Jim Bamber's aerial perspective of this wonderful track, in its pre-1995 guise, gives a graphic illustration of its elevation changes and scenic beauty, while also providing an insight into just how steely it must have been in the days before the growth of its numerous chicanes.

Amaduzzi again captures the atmosphere of the track with this startline shot of the fateful 1994 San Marino Grand Prix (above) and another view of *Tosa* as it was in 1994. To the left of the track, as it emerges from *Tamburello* and heads to the hairpin, can be seen the Santerno River, together with the reasons why sufficient run-off area was never available on the outside of the long left-hander.

Drivers gathered on the grid for a minute's silence prior to the 1995 race, to honour their fallen comrades; the approach to the revised *Tamburello* is visible in the background (above). When the race got underway it was Schumacher who led initially from pole position, followed by Berger, Coulthard, an out-of-shot Hill, Alesi and Hakkinen.

Senna *v* Prost, 1993 style, seen through Diana Burnett's camera lens. His McLaren-Ford barely a match for Prost's technologically advanced Williams-Renault (above), Senna's tactics in the early stages of that year's race drew criticism even from his most ardent supporters, but after a few high-speed frights the Frenchman clinched another victory. One year later, in that cataclysmic 1994 event, Formula One lost the gentle Ratzenberger on the Saturday, and the great Senna a day later, and nothing was ever the same again.

Roland Ratzenberger
1962-1994

Ayrton Senna
1960-1994

Echoes of Imola. Daniele Amaduzzi's wonderful aerial shot places the *Autodromo Enzo e Dino Ferrari* into its geographic perspective, with *Tosa* in the foreground amid the warm countryside of Imola.

Prost's days with Ferrari were bitter-sweet. After their near-miss in the 1990 Championship, the 1991 San Marino Grand Prix was utterly catastrophic as he spun out on the green flag lap. It wasn't much better for team-mate Jean Alesi, who had to endure the *tifosi*'s catcalls after spinning into ignominious retirement after a few laps.

The 1992 race belonged, like so many that year, to Mansell and the peerless Williams-Renault FW14B with its highly effective active suspension (above), but perhaps the happiest man in Imola that year was Martin Brundle (below). After hitting rock bottom on the Friday, following yet another run-in with Alesi, the Benetton pilot out-drove team-mate Michael Schumacher to bolster his battered confidence with an excellent fourth place. Both photographs were taken by Nigel Snowdon.

After fighting his way past Pierluigi Martini's awkward Minardi, Damon Hill fended off challenges from team-mate David Coulthard and *tifosi* darling Jean Alesi, as Mimmo Schiattarella's lapped Simtek follows. The Briton went on to an emotional victory for the Williams team, a triumph that he was able to share with the two Ferrari drivers . . .

enough Shell into the fuel pick-up to get to the *Variante Bassa*, where the same thing happened again. Piquet, having set the fastest lap on the 57th tour, was closing fast, but was nowhere near close enough, unless... Prost's frantic yawing got the McLaren just enough momentum to stagger across the line with just over seven seconds to spare over Piquet. It was a quite remarkable *tour de force*, for where others had either used too much fuel, or begun to push hard again too late, he had judged his entire race to absolute perfection.

Berger caught the slowing McLaren on the final corner, and nothing summarized the nonsense of the formula better than the sight of the Austrian braking frantically to avoid unlapping himself and thus having to complete another lap, which might have seen him also run out of fuel. In fact, had he been able to complete another lap, there was the possibility of him taking second place in the event of Piquet running out, or if Prost had not made the finishing line. And even if he had run out himself, his third place would have been safe because Johansson was still a lap behind the McLaren at the end and thus couldn't have caught the Benetton.

It was precisely such semantics which dulled the racing at that time. Too many ifs and maybes; they were not what the race fans wanted to know about. They wanted to see races where the drivers were going at it hammer-and-tongs throughout, and where the performances they saw were real. Who really knew, as they watched, whether Senna was leading by a country mile because he was genuinely quick, or because he was prepared to push into fuel debt? Who knew whether Prost was being blown off, or was merely being smart enough to have the last laugh?

Jo Ramirez makes an interesting point when summarizing the fuel economy era: "That ability that Alain had to judge a race was just fantastic, and it was something that later on Ayrton started to inherit from Alain, in 1993. It was one of the things that even Ayrton would admit, that he did learn a lot from Alain when he first started driving for us at McLaren. But in 1984 and 1985 it was hard for him. He just wanted to be the lion..."

And Dennis also made a valid observation. "Drivers sort of come into Formula One, the great ones, with raw talent and aggressivity, and total commitment and bravado, and as they get more race wins and more experience, they start to understand that you don't have to win at the highest speed, and suddenly that commitment and 'go for it' approach starts to back off a bit. They start to understand more the consequences of their actions. They still keep the performance up by using their heads and car conservation techniques. Alain was very good at that."

Later, when Fate partnered them at McLaren, we would all see just how well both Alain and Ayrton had taken on board the hard lessons of the mid-Eighties.

THE DAY SENNA FAILED TO QUALIFY

Only once in his entire Formula One career did Ayrton Senna fail to qualify, and that was at Imola in 1984, for his fourth Grand Prix, when events were taken out of his hands.

He had never driven at the track before, and was thus stunned on Friday morning when team manager Peter Gethin arrived and told the mechanics that the cars were not to be allowed out on to the track. Toleman was owed a sum of money by Pirelli, for testing work it had carried out, and team boss Alex Hawkridge had instructed Gethin that the cars must not run if the money hadn't been forthcoming.

Gethin, the winner of history's fastest Grand Prix in a BRM at Monza in 1971, and a past Formula Two race winner at Imola, recalled: "It was something I inherited when I joined the company, and it went on and on and on. I think it was probably half a dozen of one and six of another, and that was that the Italians were slow in paying and Tolemans were chasing the money because they needed it, that sort of thing.

"Anyway, on the night before the first practice I had a phone call from Alex Hawkridge in London, which I took in a kiosk in the hotel; they didn't have phones in the rooms. Unless the money was forthcoming in the morning, then we were not to run the cars. Which, as you can imagine, was a nightmare. So, knowing this, I got hold of our public relations man, Chris Witty, and said: 'Chris, it's going to be a nightmare in the morning. I need you to be there early to fend off journalists, and all that sort of thing.' So the next morning arrived, I duly went to the circuit, stopped the mechanics from allowing the cars out on the circuit, and everyone was rushing around, except that Chris didn't arrive because he was scared; he didn't show up until lunchtime. Our sponsors, of course, were Italian: Segafredo, Candy...

"There were lots of phone calls going backwards and forwards, and eventually Bernie Ecclestone stepped in and said: 'Well, let's see if we can't do something.' And he spoke with Alex and it was then, I think, after the first day, that the cars would run for the second practice."

Gethin's position can be imagined, for the Italian press went into action against Toleman, for whom he was effectively the sole representative, since Hawkridge remained in Britain. The British press was restless for information, too, and did not take kindly to a Toleman release which attempted to suggest that there was no dispute with Pirelli.

On top of it all, word got around that the team was going to change to Michelin for the next race anyway, which only heightened Italian feeling. Then, to cap it all, Senna's Hart engine developed a misfire, and his best lap of 1m 41.585s, which was completely unrepresentative of his and the TG183B's true potential, was insufficient to qualify.

"All the mechanics were pretty perplexed," Gethin continued. "I think they knew what it was about, but they just stood there. No-one wanted really to take responsibility, that's the truth. Cecotto was a little less difficult than Senna, because that's the way he was. But Senna wasn't very pleased; he was obviously very upset about it. He knew what he wanted, even before he first arrived in England, I think..." And it very definitely was not this sort of badly handled public washing of dirty laundry, with innocent parties having to bear the brunt of the argument...

Witty also recalls the incident. "Alex had decided on the tactic of not going to Imola, and had called me as well as Peter the night before. And perhaps it was right that Peter should bear the brunt of it. After all, he was the team manager! And yes, I did get to the circuit late; I didn't agree with the way Alex wanted to do it, but I had to wait for another call from him to figure how to handle the press.

"I thought it was all totally unnecessary. There had been an opportunity to go to Michelin at Zolder, but the 184 wasn't ready and Alex wanted it to be totally competitive. The 183B wasn't going to be competitive on Michelins and he didn't think it would have served any particular benefit to switch so soon. Ayrton, of course, desperately wanted to run the Michelins at Zolder. He was very unhappy with the car there and reckoned he'd do two laps and then have to pull in because it was so heavy to drive. Then the bugger just kept going round and round and finished sixth in the race after Stefan Bellof was kicked out; actually, that was a mega drive.

"At Imola Alex wanted to embarrass Pirelli publicly, which being as this was Italy and Pirelli is Italian was really clever. Anyhow, I arrived mid-morning and the shit had hit the fan. I think we only had the tyres we'd brought down with us. When Ayrton didn't qualify he and I got straight into the hire car and drove to Milan, but we couldn't get a flight out so we got another car and drove straight to Dijon. It was while talking with him on that journey that I began to get a hint of the frustration he was feeling at Toleman."

By the French Grand Prix at Dijon Toleman had introduced its new TG184 and switched to Michelin tyres, and two races on from Imola Senna drove like a master to finish second to Prost at Monaco. As an intriguing aside, Witty added: "And don't forget that we still only got the second division Michelins, whereas McLaren and whomever had the really good stuff. Michel Dupasquier at Michelin always thought that Ayrton was absolutely mega on tyres..."

But right then all that was still in the future, and Imola left a bad taste all round.

"It was a pretty nasty old business, really," Gethin summarized. "It was a pretty difficult episode that took a nice taste away from Imola. I used to think it was such a nice place."

9
Commerce takes a back seat

"Brain damage, foot damage, it doesn't make much difference. You're not fit to drive." – Prof Watkins to Nelson Piquet

It was the blisters that were the problem. Imola has always been a delicate trade-off of downforce against the need for as much maximum speed as possible to haul a car out of the tight corner before the pits and keep it on full song all the way through *Tamburello* and on down that long, long run to *Tosa*. Too much drag meant not only reduced speeds here, where it mattered a great deal, but also increased fuel consumption which, as we have seen, was always such a critical factor.

But in 1987, as teams sifted through the data gathered during the Friday morning's free practice for the San Marino Grand Prix, there were clear suggestions that in some cases insufficient downforce was letting some of the quicker cars slide around too much, which in turn was hurting the rear tyres. Goodyear's engineers wore puzzled frowns. The blisters on the centre of the tread were, perhaps, to be expected, but those on the inside were not.

The Akron giant faced an interesting problem at this, the second race of the season, for with Pirelli's withdrawal at the end of 1986 it had once again had thrust upon it the role of sole supplier of Formula One rubber. The production of tyres for all of the Formula One teams as well as for Indianapolis had stretched the company's facilities and had put it under a lot of pressure. One consequence was that the tyres it had brought to Imola were of a slightly earlier construction than those which had been supplied for the previous week's testing.

During that morning session, Williams' big problem had not been tyres, however, for almost alone the team was able to run sufficient downforce. Instead, it was traffic, Nigel Mansell in particular complaining vociferously about the speed differential between his FW11B and some of the normally aspirated cars which, that year, were running for two subsidiary awards, the lamentably named Jim Clark Cup for drivers and Colin Chapman Cup for constructors. Given the second-best nature of these silly 'Championships', one could imagine Jimmy and 'Chunky' looking down with serious frowns on their faces.

"I just don't think they realize the closing speed of the turbos... I know what it's like. I mean, it's only five years since I was driving a normally aspirated car in amongst other people's turbos," Mansell told Alan Henry at *Motoring News*. "During the untimed session I was almost alongside a couple of them when they just saw me in time to avoid turning into me..." Back in 1980, of course, he had lost his own chance of qualifying when he had crashed his Lotus 81B while moving over for one of the Ligiers, so this was no idle whinge.

As usual, there had been further rule changes for the 1987 season. The fuel allowance remained at 195 litres, but for the first time FISA had made an attempt to limit turbo horsepower; it was the first step of the phasing-out of forced-induction engines pending a new 3.5-litre normally aspirated Formula One for 1989. FISA achieved this limitation by means of the famous pop-off valve, which was supposed to dump boost when it exceeded 4-bar, or four times ambient barometric pressure. The Benetton-BMW of 1986 has generally been accepted as the highwater mark for Formula One power outputs with 1,300bhp, but Jabby Crombac subsequently has disclosed that the highest figure Renault could calculate for qualifying boost – like everyone else's, its dynamometer only went to 1,000bhp, so it had to extrapolate – was a truly staggering 1,650... Whatever, such monsters were now creatures of a bygone era. As the season progressed, however, there would be suggestions that various engine manufacturers (principally Honda) had found a way of over-blowing the valve to achieve a little more than that for qualifying. And interestingly, 4-bar was actually a little more than quite a few teams had dared to run in races during 1986.

This, allied to further improvements in fuel efficiency and engine management electronics, would not only result in further cuts in lap times, despite the horsepower reduction, but would largely eliminate the pathetic sight of cars with empty fuel tanks rolling to a halt within sight of the chequered flag.

Formula One thus got a major new lease of life in 1987, and there was some cracking racing. And as Mansell found at Imola, on acceleration out of the corner before the pits the turbocars were still pulling some 20mph more across the start/finish line than their normally aspirated brethren.

All that, however, became academic when Nelson Piquet began his seventh lap of qualifying. A little earlier he had set what would be the day's fastest lap of 1m 25.997s, and he was now embarked upon his seventh consecutive lap of the session. He overtook the tardy Adrian Campos in the Minardi and had entered *Tamburello* when disaster struck.

On the exit of the long curve, his Williams-Honda FW11B suddenly spun and struck the concrete outer wall backwards at enormous speed.

Teo Fabi had also been close by in his Benetton, and on entering the pits at the end of his lap he immediately told the Williams crew: "You'd better get down there as quickly as possible. Nelson is out of the car, but he's lying on the grass..."

It was one of those moments when the pit lane goes very quiet, but the emergency services had been on the scene with great alacrity, and gradually news filtered through that, though bruised and shaken, the Brazilian was going to be okay. It would later transpire that the left rear tyre had failed going into *Tamburello*. The right rear, which bore the greatest load through that corner, was still inflated when the wreckage was later examined.

"My memory is that the car spun round and went into the wall backwards on the left rear corner, but then the left front corner impacted on the wall as well," said Williams' technical director Patrick Head. "Certainly the suspension completely collapsed and the wheel shattered, and it actually drove the upright through the side of the monocoque round about the footwell area where Nelson's ankles and feet were. But though it did go through the monocoque around about the suspension bulkheads towards the front, and displaced them a little, it didn't go through enough to damage his legs. It was a very, very big impact, but the main structure of the monocoque was intact.

"It was a tyre that failed. That was a period where, basically, because we were running such enormous horsepower, we were able to run enormous wings on the cars and we were producing massive downforce. I'm not sure that either we maybe hadn't given Goodyear quite the scale of figures involved, or Goodyear hadn't been testing at the loading levels, but whatever it was concerned the sidewalls of the tyres.

"It was basically a repeat of what happened to Nigel in Adelaide in 1986. And we had also had a couple of tyres fail on us over the winter, and we were saying to Goodyear, please do something about it, please do something about it. And I wouldn't say they did nothing, but I think their response was not really strong enough, and it wasn't until Nelson's accident at Imola that they realized the problem was quite as big as it was."

Despite the reduction in qualifying boost pressure, the latest cars were still pumping out a great deal of power. "I would imagine we were 900, 950, something like that," Head estimates. "Quite a lot, anyway." Certainly it was enough not only to impose significant loadings on the tyres, but to enable the team to run very high downforce, which further increased the loadings. At this time Williams enjoyed a huge power advantage with the Honda V6 and was able to run markedly higher downforce than anybody else. In later years, Head would suggest that the team had the same sort of advantage then that it would enjoy with the active FW14B in 1992.

As Piquet was taken first to the medical centre at the track, and then to Bologna for a routine brain scan, Goodyear quickly took stock of the situation. It immediately limited every runner to only four-lap runs for the remainder of the session. Meanwhile, it did a stock-take on the test tyres left back at its Wolverhampton base, and some that were still at the Ferrari factory, and calculated that there were sufficient to supply each team with nine sets between two cars. The blistered tyres were withdrawn.

In a slick piece of work, Goodyear chartered a BAC 1-11, which picked up the new batch of tyres once they'd been trucked from Wolverhampton to Kent, and they arrived in Bologna in time for Saturday. As a bonus, the drivers soon found that they didn't blister, and they also offered more grip and more consistent behaviour. "I don't think there was a massive change between the normal tyres and the test tyres," Head recalls, "but there certainly was a change to the structure. I think they had added a ply or two."

Nelson's lap time stood as fastest for the rest of the day, and as untimed practice began on Saturday morning, the battered Brazilian turned up for work after discharging himself from hospital. The scene was set for an angry and frank exchange of views between him and Professor Sid Watkins, then the leading neurological surgeon from the Royal London Hospital as well as being the FIA's medical chief, and Imola's Italian doctors. Piquet was not allowed to drive in that session, but the argument rumbled on as official qualifying came around.

"Nelson first of all wanted to race, and certainly Prof said 'No'," said Head. "I think Nelson had been talking gobbledygook – not that he necessarily didn't talk gobbledygook when he was otherwise! – but he had certainly had the most enormous impact. I would say that it subdued him for a bit. It was a physical thing rather than a mental thing. I think it literally subdued him. It was a very, very big thump."

Williams engineer Frank Dernie, subsequently with Ligier, did some calculations on the accident. "It was a fairly shallow angle, similar to Senna's, I should think. Like Nelson, Ayrton should just have been shaken; but he was unlucky. Nelson wasn't that coherent afterwards, but then again, he wasn't always that coherent!"

Prof Watkins, the man at the centre of what would become a highly important test case for Formula One, stood his ground firmly in the face of great pressure to allow Piquet to compete. Nelson's personal physician, Dr Raphael Grajales-Robles, agreed with Prof, but understandably, Bernie Ecclestone and the organizers were extremely keen not to lose a key gate draw.

"Nelson was out of the car by the time I arrived, a bit stunned," Watkins recollected. "He didn't quite know where he was to begin with, but we took him to the medical centre and by then he knew who he was, where he was, and what he was doing. He went off in the helicopter to the hospital in Bologna, where there's a neuro-surgical unit, and he had a brain scan and then stayed overnight.

"The next morning he discharged himself, so I wasn't surprised to hear from Bernie when I arrived that he wanted to drive. Anyway, he came to see me, and I said to him that he couldn't drive because he'd had a head injury and he might have some brain damage. And he said: 'No, he hadn't got any brain damage.' So I said: 'Well, why have you left your shoe off?' He only had one shoe on. So he said: 'It's not because I forgot it, but because my foot is so painful and swollen I can't get a shoe on.'

"I said: 'Brain damage, foot damage, it doesn't make much difference. You're not fit to drive.'

"So then there was a bit of pressure from the circuit people, about wanting him to drive, and I think Bernie probably wanted him to drive. The chap who stayed right out of the argument was old Balestre, for which I gave him credit. Nelson didn't drive in the morning practice, and then there was some talk that he was going to be allowed to make some demonstration runs between the two practices, and if he went all right in that then he could participate in the Saturday afternoon qualifying practice. That upset all the Italian doctors, and me, and the chief medical officer, who had got a statement from the neuro-surgeon who had looked after him overnight, said that there was no way the medical staff would see him either demonstrate or drive, and maintain their responsibility for the circuit. So it became an impasse, really, and thereafter the pressure for him to drive sort of disappeared."

Prof Watkins himself had been quite prepared to resign, head home and watch the race on television had things reached a head, and that would have been a long-term disaster for Formula One. Fortunately, commonsense prevailed.

"I think the Italian papers made a good deal of the fact that I'd prevented Nelson from driving so that Nigel, who was in the same team, could get an advantage... Nelson later admitted – some months later – in some article I saw, that he wasn't himself for about three months after the shunt. He couldn't sleep and he wasn't on form. So in retrospect, he thought I'd been quite right, although at the time he was pretty upset. He cried a bit, and that sort of thing. But he didn't bad-mouth me."

Thierry Boutsen later had a similar impact in a Williams while testing in Rio, and like Piquet he escaped virtually unharmed as testimony to the inherent integrity of the Williams chassis. But again like the Brazilian, he too would find that he was not fully himself for three months or more.

Thus Imola 1987 became something of a watershed, the prototype for all other similar situations, the confirmation that, unlikely though it might seem, something really did exist which could actually override the commercial considerations of the day. And that something was the medical side of Formula One. Since then, Prof Watkins's word has been taken as law.

"I suppose so," he admitted recently. "But it was before. This, I think, was a sort of test of whether or not the medical advice could overcome the commercial value. And in the past perhaps the commercial value hadn't been serious enough, so I didn't have the contest, if you see what I mean. When Nigel banged his head in Ricard, in 1985, he didn't want to race the next day, so he went home instead. When other famous people, like Niki, hurt his wrist, he was sensible enough at Spa to say he didn't want to drive.

"It was one of those things, I suppose. Here was this crowd at Imola, with a big following for Piquet, and the removal of him from that particular competition reduced its hype value. He and Nigel were hard at it for the Championship, of course, but equity was restored later in the year when Nigel missed Suzuka because he hurt his back. And Adelaide, too. As it turned out it was almost one each, effectively, and I felt all right about it."

Thankfully, there were no more accidents that weekend. Though Ayrton Senna narrowly beat Mansell to pole position in the active Lotus 99T, the Briton had the race in his pocket from the second lap and simply stormed away to a victory which confirmed to sceptics that the tyre failure which had cost him the World Championship in Australia the previous year had done nothing to quench his competitive fires.

Alain Prost, always a serious threat in the McLaren, retired with alternator failure after only 15 laps when he was happily stroking along not far behind the Williams-Honda, and though Michele Alboreto set *tifosi* hearts beating by leading during the routine pit stops, nothing came close to interrupting Mansell's flow that afternoon. Senna fought off the Ferrari's strong challenge in the final stages to finish second, almost half a minute behind, with Stefan Johansson fourth for McLaren after a stop to replace a broken front wing endplate. Martin Brundle scored the Zakspeed team's first World Championship points, and Satoru Nakajima was sixth in the other Lotus.

One of the strongest performances came from Riccardo Patrese, in the sharp-looking Brabham BT56, which the Italian pushed into second place on two occasions. The first was when his crew let him stay out as Mansell, Senna and Alboreto all made their first stops, but the second came just as Alboreto had pulled off a great move by diving inside the Lotus going into *Acque Minerali*; as Ayrton missed a gear in the excitement, Riccardo slipped by both of them at the *Variante Alta* chicane. For a while it seemed that he might finally be about to lay the ghost of 1983, but from the 50th of the race's 59 laps his BMW engine began misfiring as the alternator functioned inconsistently. Riccardo would have to wait another three years for the gods to smile.

A FIRST FOR JAPAN

Others had tried before, notably Masahiro Hasemi, Kazuyoshi Hoshino and Noritake Takahara, but Satoru Nakajima finally succeeded in Imola where his other countrymen had failed by becoming the first Japanese driver ever to score a World Championship point.

Williams had long resisted being 'advised' on its driver line-up by its engine supplier, but Lotus had no such qualms and needed the financial support that Naka brought with him. On top of that, the little driver was perfectly suited as a team-mate to Ayrton Senna, for he would offer no challenge, nor make any waves that might detract from the effort put into the number one car.

'Nakajap', as he was known affectionately in the pit lane, qualified a respectable 12th, albeit almost four seconds off the pace of his team-mate, but he very nearly didn't make the race when his active suspension 'sat down' as the battery failed during the first pre-race warm-up lap. Frantic action by the Lotus team got Senna's spare car ready for him, but it took a slice of good luck to make up for this misfortune.

As the race was about to start without him, Martin Brundle, Thierry Boutsen and Eddie Cheever all stalled on the grid, necessitating a five-minute delay (which also knocked a lap off the scheduled distance to obviate the need to top up fuel tanks again). This allowed Nakajima to start from the pit lane, with pedal and wheel settings hastily juggled from Senna's preference. Then, just as he was being wheeled to the end of the pit road, mechanics discovered that one of the tyres was deflating...

After all that drama Nakajima finally did go to the ball, and in a solid performance he pulled up through the field to take sixth place. By the flag he had closed significantly on Brundle, whose Zakspeed had boiled away its brake fluid. It was only Nakajima's second Grand Prix.

10
God is my co-pilot

"I remember thinking: 'I'm not sure I want to drive one of these things again...' but by the time I was in the ambulance I began wondering whether I might be fit enough to race at Monaco..." – Gerhard Berger

They were McLaren-Honda years, 1988 and 1989, at Imola. Years when, on both occasions, Ayrton Senna took pole position with team-mate Alain Prost alongside him; and when they finished first and second, in that order, both times. Years when the red and white steamroller proved unstoppable, no matter what its rivals tried to do. But they were also much more than that, for it was at Imola that the seeds of enmity between Senna and Prost would truly flourish after a disagreement in the 1989 San Marino Grand Prix.

1989 would also be the race in which the spectre of death visited Formula One for the first time since 1986, and when the sport found itself once again celebrating the deliverance of another son after a truly miraculous escape.

But in 1988, Gerhard Berger's fiery accident was a long way into the future as the new-look Formula One rolled into the *Autodromo Dino Ferrari* in what would be the last year of Enzo Ferrari's life. This was also to be the last year of the turbocharged engines, and many teams, including Benetton, Ligier, Minardi and the minor leaguers, had already made the switch to cheaper, normally aspirated Cosworth DFR or Judd CV power. Williams, too, faced a transitional season with duller colours in its paintbox as a result of Honda's defection to McLaren, the Didcot team partnering Nigel Mansell and Riccardo Patrese as they relied on John Judd's development CV engines in the hope that a nimble, unblown car might be able to beat the more powerful, but much thirstier turbos.

The latter faced a tricky year, for fuel allowance had been slashed yet again, this time from 195 litres to a mere 150, and boost was down from 4-bar to a measly 2.5-bar. Benetton, and Ford in particular, took the easy option and junked the promising 1.5-litre V6, thereby depriving Formula One of a unit which many believed might well have been the perfect engine for the year, and McLaren-Honda of what might have been its only serious opposition. This was taken as a sign of Ford's reluctance to take Formula One seriously any more, especially as Benetton had to rely on the resuscitated DFR engine while an all-new HB V8 took shape for 1989. Honda and Ferrari, however, were prepared to make the necessary commitment, and they invested many thousands of dollars modifying their existing turbo engines. In a year when McLaren and Honda would win 15 of the 16 races, and would only lose at Monza because of Senna's problem with backmarker Jean-Louis Schlesser, whom he was attempting to lap, it was brutally clear which team had done its homework best.

Nevertheless, at Imola there were many who simply were not prepared to believe that McLaren-Honda could get the job done on a circuit where fuel economy was so important, and Ron Dennis and his men, though they ran it close at times, delighted in proving them wrong.

In practice, Senna continued to prove that he was quicker than Prost when outright speed mattered, by taking yet another pole position in 1m 27.148s to his partner's 1m 27.919s. Lotus was still using the Honda turbo, too, but Nelson Piquet was light years away in his new berth as he rattled off a lap in 1m 30.500s to take third place. Alessandro Nannini was fourth for Benetton on his home ground, followed by Berger and Patrese, and then Eddie Cheever's Arrows with its Megatron (*nee* BMW) turbo. Thierry Boutsen was eighth in the second Benetton, just in front of Ivan Capelli's attractive new March and a Michele Alboreto who would become increasingly disenchanted with his lot at Ferrari. As luck would have it, Michele would have to start from the back of the grid after a dragging clutch caused him to stall on the warm-up lap.

Right from the start the race came to Senna as Prost's engine died when the lights went green; he'd reported it fluffing on the warm-up lap, via his two-way radio. As Senna stormed away, Piquet came through into second place and at the end of the lap the two Brazilians led from Patrese, Nannini, Berger, Prost, Cheever, Capelli, Boutsen and Mansell, the latter starting only 11th after struggling throughout qualifying with his Williams FW12's troublesome 'reactive' suspension.

That was all anyone really saw of Senna for the rest of the afternoon, but Piquet would have his hands full. To rub in the domination of the McLarens, Prost caught and passed the Lotus after only eight laps, but by then Senna had 8.1 seconds in hand, and though Alain might have had the advantage on conservation of his machinery, Ayrton's awesome ability to cut through traffic without losing momentum would keep that particular equation in balance. Piquet, an embarrassing three seconds a lap slower than the red and white cars, was already having to consider his fuel situation. Later he would reveal that he'd driven the whole way to third place with one eye on his readout.

It was left to Nannini, Patrese, Boutsen and Berger to provide what meagre thrills the crowd had that day, with some fine wheel-to-wheel racing for a while. Mansell became involved, too, despite an overheating engine, and when Nannini spun at *Tosa* on the 36th lap the Briton had a chance to attack his old enemy, Piquet. He actually got the Williams ahead of the Lotus on lap 40, but two laps later his engine cut out. Patrese, too, hit trouble, with erratic handling and loss of power because of a cracked exhaust. Boutsen thus hounded Piquet to the flag, with Nannini recovering to finish sixth behind a subdued Berger.

To the despair of the *tifosi*, the race was a disaster for Ferrari, which couldn't even muster Lotus speed, let alone consider challenging the McLarens. The V6 turbo had been wound down so much in the interests of fuel economy that Berger complained afterwards that he had had no power throughout the race. He did at least have reliability, however; Alboreto had driven through to eighth place despite a similar handicap, only to suffer engine failure five laps from the end.

Take the McLarens away, and it had been one hell of a race, with passing and repassing and some very determined driving. At the end, the quartet of cars between third and sixth places was separated by less than seven seconds. But the McLarens were there, and the San Marino Grand Prix provided them with a perfect opportunity for another emphatic demonstration. This time there were to be no last-minute dramas with low fuel or underweight cars, and they had ruled the day, even though they had been obliged to use far less fuel than they had struggled by with two years earlier. Run hard, roll it off, sprint at the end if the readouts are right; the lessons of the mid-Eighties had indeed been well learned. The rest of the field was completely stunned.

Furthermore, any thoughts that McLaren-Honda's decision to run with turbos in 1988 might have lost the two companies the year's valuable experience which had been gained by other teams through changing over to normally aspirated engines 12 months before they absolutely had to, were soon to be dashed when the new formula was introduced for 1989.

A lot had changed by the time the circus rolled back into Imola. Enzo Ferrari had died the previous August and the circuit had been renamed the *Autodromo Enzo e Dino Ferrari*. Nigel Mansell had left Williams to join Berger at Ferrari; Boutsen had left Benetton to join Patrese at Williams in his place; the Brabham team was back with Martin Brundle and Stefano Modena; and the hugely promising British driver Johnny Herbert had fought back from shattering his ankles in a massive accident in the Formula 3000 race at Brands Hatch in August 1988, to join Alessandro Nannini at Benetton.

For all that, as soon as practice got under way it became clear enough that the yardsticks would remain the same. Senna and Prost would front the grid, and as usual their lap times were well below anyone else's. Senna recorded 1m 26.010s to Prost's 1m 26.235s; Mansell was the closest with 1m 27.652s ahead of Patrese, Berger, Boutsen, Nannini and Piquet.

Mansell had won the opening race of the year in Brazil, a victory which had come completely against all expectation since the sleek new Ferrari had been in all sorts of reliability problems during pre-season testing. Now, the *tifosi*, which had caused church bells to be rung throughout Italy on the evening of that dramatic success, was praying for a similar miracle. But instead, they were to see a miracle of a different kind visited upon the other Ferrari.

A colleague and I were watching down at the entry to *Traguardo*, as was our wont in those days, before watching races on the television monitors became almost mandatory. We saw how big Senna's lead was at the end of the first lap, and we watched him lead Prost, Mansell, Patrese, Berger and Boutsen by our viewing spot. Later, we would watch on the monitor replays and learn just how unruly the pack had been as it jostled its way down to *Tosa* at the start, with wheel-banging that, a little further on, would pitch Mauricio Gugelmin's March on to the grass at *Acque Minerali*.

And then, just as the leaders had streamed by us to finish their fourth lap and commence their fifth, we heard the commentators' voices reach a fresh pitch, and from our limited understanding of Italian we pieced together that Berger had gone off at *Tamburello* in a sizeable accident. Back at the pits, the true horror quickly became apparent. That, and the fact that fire had returned to Formula One. Looking back, even now, I can remember how totally shocking that seemed, for it was a spectre we all believed had been banished for good.

Gerhard had been pushing hard after Patrese, and in turn he had the second Williams right on his gearbox. But then the Ferrari simply didn't make the second part of the *Tamburello* curve. Instead, it just kept running wider and wider until it struck the concrete outer wall at an oblique angle before slithering down it for 300 yards and shedding bodywork as it went. It gouged grass and dirt into a dust cloud, and then suddenly this white cloud was tinged by a horrible orange ball of flame.

Incredibly, the rescue workers went into action even as the Ferrari was going on to the grass at high speed, in a fantastic piece of reaction. The fire intervention car was there within 15 seconds, arriving at the same time as three marshals – Bruno Miniati, Paolo Verdi and Gabriele Vivoli – who were already known as the 'Angels of Imola' after helping Nelson Piquet there two years earlier. But on that occasion Nelson had been able to take his time. Now the situation was critical, and undoubtedly the Angels saved Gerhard's life.

Within 23 seconds the fire had been contained. By the time the race had been red-flagged and Gerhard had been extracted and whisked away to the medical centre, he was already seen to be giving the *tifosi* the thumbs-up. The paddock was wreathed in unalloyed smiles as the news of his well-being filtered through.

How lucky had he been? Williams stayed on to test at the circuit, and the day after Berger's miraculous escape engineer Frank Dernie took some measurements and made some calculations.

"I measured the skid marks, relative to the wall, and he was at a sort of 30 to 35 degrees oblique angle, so it was the equivalent to a head-on of probably 40mph or so. You have to guess to a certain extent because you don't know how much he was decelerating. It could have been less. But we know that a 40mph head-on accident into a concrete wall, and you're dead. There's almost nothing that can be done for you.

"So these accidents at very, very high speeds are luckily at oblique angles and the car goes skidding and spidering down the track, dissipating energy over a very considerable period of time. They look spectacular, but the peak Gs aren't that high. The very bad accidents are the ones that are over in fractions of a second."

But what had caused the shunt? Tyre failure was quickly ruled out, and the focus turned to some sort of breakage in the car itself. But what? Later, Boutsen would describe how he had seen one of the Ferrari's front wings go flying off just before the impact. John Barnard's analysis was as painstaking as one would expect, assuming that one knew as much about the subject as the English designer. In the end he concluded: "The drivers had been subjecting the front wings to forces with which they had not been designed to cope."

He believed that a front wing had sheared at its root as a result of continual impacts as Berger ran over kerbs, something that Barnard had tried to discourage his drivers from doing. The wings had actually been stiffened slightly for 1989, and this in turn had reduced their tolerance of the sort of deflections that running over kerbs was putting them through. When the wing sheared as Gerhard was going through *Tamburello*, there was nothing he could do about the sudden, and terminal, understeer. Like Senna, he would be carried into the wall, but unlike Ayrton, luck rode with him.

He was extracted within seconds from the burning chassis, and after Prof Watkins and his crew had struggled to subdue him, within minutes he was being examined in the medical centre and undergoing the usual scans and X-rays. He was then transferred to the Maggiore Hospital in Bologna, having sustained nothing worse than a broken rib, a fractured shoulder blade, some painful chemical burns to his body, burns to his palms and a severe shaking. Predictably, he discharged himself in the morning, and had himself flown home to Innsbruck for further treatment.

We were surprised to bump into him in the Loews Hotel in Monaco a fortnight later, when each of us fought back the natural impulse to try and shake his heavily bandaged hands. He'd been watching out on the circuit that day, and he was cheerful.

"But I just told Derek Warwick: 'I'd rather be in it, driving it, than out there watching. It looks bloody scary!'"

Imola was already receding, and he was his usual jokey self. "I remember thinking that a front tyre had failed, so I went hard on the brakes until I left the track. Then I took my hands off the wheel, tucked them under my armpits and pulled my legs up as far as I could. For the first few minutes after the impact I remember thinking: 'I'm not sure I want to drive one of these things again...' but by the time I was in the ambulance I began wondering whether I might be fit enough to race at Monaco..."

The race was restarted after an argument on the grid between FISA's Roland Bruynseraede and representatives from Williams, Ligier and Dallara. The red flags stopping the race had only been displayed at the final corner, so cars were lined up on the grid as they stopped. Under the rules they could only be worked on in the pit lane, but none had been allowed to enter it.

Boutsen's car had sustained a puncture, almost certainly from debris. Alex Caffi's Dallara had collided with Olivier Grouillard's Ligier, an easy enough thing to do with the Frenchman, and both cars needed attention. But Roland wasn't playing ball and told them all they'd have to push their cars into the pit road and start from there. It was not exactly fair, even if that's what the rules said.

This time Prost led as far as *Tosa*, where Senna grabbed the initiative and sped off to another win, but though his team-mate eventually finished 40 seconds in arrears, Prost had been on one of his deceptively quick charges, and by third-distance was within striking range. The gap was less than a second, but on the 43rd lap he was caught out by a blister on his left front tyre and spun briefly at *Variante Bassa*. He quickly recovered both his rhythm and his position, but any chance of victory had gone.

Third place would be the subject of a heated battle between Patrese, Nannini and Mansell. *Il Leone* (the lion), as the *tifosi* were already calling Mansell, was not yet sure why his team-mate's car had crashed, and it was a brave decision to drive on in ignorance, especially as Ferrari had given him the choice. Say what you will about the man's propensity to whinge at times, he drove like a hero that day and was pushing very hard after Riccardo until the Italian's Renault V10 abruptly broke on the way down to *Rivazza* on the 22nd lap. This time the *tifosi* gave him a polite cheer as they reserved their voices for Mansell, but he only had two more laps to run before his gearbox broke.

Piquet and Warwick, who was driving Ross Brawn's new Arrows A11, were also locked in battle, while further back Nicola Larini underlined his talent by pushing the little underdog Osella as high as ninth in a combat with Andrea de Cesaris' Dallara. Piquet's Lotus broke its Judd engine on lap 30, but Warwick had already been passed by Boutsen, who now lay fourth. That was the way they stayed, with the Belgian eating into Nannini's third place cushion, but failing to close the gap sufficiently. Warwick hung on for fifth, while Jonathan Palmer drove one of his best races to bring the brand new Tyrrell 018 through to sixth place from the back of the grid after a stylish drive.

Afterwards, Boutsen and Caffi were excluded from fourth and seventh places for contravening the startline rules, but they were subsequently to be reinstated.

The 1989 San Marino Grand Prix thus ended with the McLaren steamroller repeating the sort of victory that it had produced so often at Imola, and with a general mood of good cheer after Berger's escape.

But there had also been clear signs of serious aggravation in the McLaren camp, which had many tongues wagging. The seeds of discontent had bloomed, and from now on Ron Dennis would be living on borrowed time as far as his superteam driver pairing was concerned. By July, Prost would announce that he was going to Ferrari, and he and Senna prepared to take the gloves off in rival teams. Many of us thought they had been that way since 1988; only their overalls had really betrayed the fact that they were team-mates.

THE SEEDS OF DESTRUCTION

It was always going to be an uneasy relationship, as if a town's two fastest gunslingers had decided to drink whisky in the same saloon. Yet for the most part it survived 1988 with no more than one glitch, which had come at Estoril when Ayrton Senna weaved over towards Alain Prost at 180mph down the main straight as the Frenchman overtook him. That year, the Brazilian had gone on to win his first World Championship and lay claim to Prost's overall crown; by 1989 there was tension within their partnership, and it had its seeds in Imola.

The more they raced, the greater seemed the likelihood that eventually they would collide with one another, for really this was a case of the irresistible force meeting the immovable object. Senna recognized this, and at Imola he made a suggestion. Would Alain agree to a no-overtaking pact on the first lap under braking for *Tosa*?

It seemed a reasonable idea, and Prost, ever the pragmatist, agreed. After all, he'd been on the receiving end of some of Senna's overtaking moves, and he knew how ruthlessly calculated they could be. Often he had measured the allowance given to him by his 'team-mate' in millimetres.

Senna, from pole position, made the most of the race's first start and led Prost easily down to *Tosa*. The matter of overtaking was thus academic. But then had come Berger's accident.

At the restart, Senna lagged slightly, and it was Prost who just got the jump. But only as far as the approach to *Tosa*... There, Senna came drafting by to grab the lead, and that was that. Prost just sat there, livid, and stayed livid all afternoon as he drove round to finish second yet again in a controlled rage. And afterwards, in a manner so reminiscent of Gilles Villeneuve seven years earlier, he stormed away with barely a word, missing the post-race press conference.

Later, he would make the depth of his feelings clear very publicly. Senna, he believed, had duped him. Senna had suggested the no-overtaking plan, and then Senna had broken it at will. Ayrton made an attempt to justify his move, suggesting that the 'arrangement' had covered the area into *Tosa*, whereas he had overtaken his team-mate just before then. It was a moot point, and Prost was not interested in semantics.

He had a blazing row with Dennis after the race, in the team motorhome, where he reminded Ron that he had told him the previous November in Adelaide that he [Dennis] would have to take steps to ensure that Senna toed the team line. "What is the point of agreements, Ron?" Prost fumed. "We agree that we don't overtake under braking for the first corner. So what happens? Ayrton overtakes me just that way! He respects nothing for the team!"

And he told me in an interview: "I knew I had to be careful, because I well remember the story of Gilles and Didier. I was not going to do the same thing..."

All Ron would say publicly was: "It is a matter for Alain to talk about." But that didn't stop him from trying to con the press in Monte Carlo before the next race that all was sweetness and light within the team, when it was abundantly obvious that it wasn't, but you couldn't blame him for trying.

Prost then gave a blistering interview to his friends in *l'Equipe*, the influential French sports daily. "McLaren has always been loyal with me, and as far as technical discussions go I will not completely close the door," he said. "As far as Senna is concerned, I want nothing more to do with him. I have always tried to keep relationships good in the team. They were good in the past with Niki, Keke and Stefan, but I will no longer do that with Senna.

"What I appreciate more than anything is honesty. He has not been honest. Ron Dennis had to put him under a lot of pressure to get him to tell the truth. Ayrton was very upset. He even cried. It was incredible."

Senna himself refused to make any further comment, but the damage was done. The truth was that the lid was now well and truly off the simmering relationship, and the beginnings of the lengthy feud between Ayrton Senna and Alain Prost were finally out in the public domain, where they would remain until the bitter end.

11
A score is settled

"I think I was repaid all the things that happened in the past..."
– Riccardo Patrese

The 1990 San Marino Grand Prix was, almost without doubt, the pinnacle of Riccardo Patrese's career. Certainly, it was the one which made up for all the disappointments of the Imola years, when good placings had seemed imminent, only to be snatched away, but more than anything else it was the result that finally laid the ghost of 1983, when he had thrown it all away while leading comfortably with only five laps left to run.

This was a year of entrenchment for McLaren and Honda, after the Woking team had continued its domination from 1988 into 1989. The biggest challenge came from Ferrari, where the arrival of Alain Prost, though it had upset current encumbent Nigel Mansell, had undoubtedly added to the edge the resurgent team had established the previous year when the ebullient Briton had won two races. For the *tifosi* this was a time of genuine excitement, for Ferrari was back on the warpath and could be expected to challenge strongly for victory, while the Renault challenge was also growing as Williams continued work on the initially unpromising FW13.

Benetton had its B190, which was powered by a developed version of the Cosworth HB which had appeared midway through the previous season, and its chassis had largely been penned by John Barnard, the man responsible for the revival of Ferrari's fortunes. It was the Scuderia's loss that it hadn't been able to hold on to the mercurial British design guru, but that mistake would be rectified in later years.

Though Imola was its usual sunny self, there were tensions in the air. Down at McLaren, managing director Ron Dennis was still smarting after claiming that Ferrari had enticed Steve Nichols to leave his team. Though it was water under the bridge to those concerned by the time they got to Imola, this was the first time that Dennis had faced the British press since the incident and its outcome, and a certain amount of smirking and leg-pulling was inevitable.

Then there was a little incident at a dinner to which we had been invited one evening by Ferrari, at the *Ristorante Naldi*, just outside the main gates. Here, in the cool, typically Italian interior of this likable establishment, the idea was that we could get together again with the Ferrari drivers in a less frantic atmosphere than our usual ambushes in the pit lane.

When Nigel Mansell walked in he was clearly offended that the specialist press had congregated round Alain Prost at the dinner table, leaving the Fleet Streeters to await him at the other end of the room. It wasn't done out of any sense of spite; it was simply that getting hold of Prost most other times was far more difficult than getting hold of Mansell, and the opportunity to sit down with him, in company with some of our Italian media friends, was too good to resist. Mansell, I am sure, did not see things that way. The Briton, however, would be the star turn of the weekend, Patrese's victory notwithstanding.

Senna, inevitably, dominated qualifying and took pole position for McLaren in 1m 23.220s, sharing the front row with his new team-mate, Gerhard Berger, who was beginning to find his feet in his new environment. Patrese and Boutsen were on the second row for Williams, with the Ferraris on the third. Mansell just edged out Prost, while the future Ferrari star, Jean Alesi, was an impressive seventh for Tyrrell in the car which would really kickstart the trend towards very high noses. That wily campaigner, Nelson Piquet, was eighth fastest for Benetton.

Goodyear had Pirelli again as opposition on the tyre front, and thus its runners had a choice of compounds for the race. The McLaren drivers went for the softer C compound on the left and harder Bs on the right, Prost went for Bs all round, and Mansell, ever the gambler, plumped for Cs.

It was Berger who led at the start from Senna, but when he missed a gear on the run to *Tosa*, both Senna and Boutsen went by and Gerhard had to watch as Ayrton took his customary place at the head of the pack. Further back, Mansell was driving like a man who'd had a bang on the head, which, oddly enough, was precisely what he was. Unwittingly, he had walked into the partially raised ramp of a transporter and given himself a nasty gash that needed stitching before the off. Perhaps that was why he got *Tamburello* wrong and spat dirt at his team-mate as he put a wheel on the grass during the adrenalin rush of the opening lap. Behind him, Nakajima wrote his Tyrrell off in a sizeable collision with Capelli's Leyton House as a result of this debris, and when Alesi made one of his opportunistic moves on Mansell at *Tosa* moments later, Prost was on the receiving end as he was elbowed into the dirt again. Throw in Martin Donnelly getting away with a complete 360-degree spin at the hairpin, in the middle of the pack, and it made for quite an adventurous first lap!

Senna looked strong in the lead with all this nonsense going on behind him, but on lap four he slowed suddenly on the run down to *Rivazza*, before slithering dramatically into the sand trap on the outside. It was one of the most bizarre reasons for retirement in a long time, for a stone had lodged itself inside one of his rear brake calipers and had literally machined its way through the right rear wheel rim, hence the problem he had making the corner.

That left the race wide open, and Berger looked the best bet for victory at this stage since few expected Boutsen's leading Williams-Renault to have sufficient pace to resist the McLaren-Honda. The Belgian was driving with the precision and consistency that was his hallmark, however, and was still holding his advantage when he pitted on lap 18. He'd missed a gearchange due to a problem selecting third gear, and when he found first gear instead the Renault V10 had succumbed to the wildly excessive revs.

If Berger thought he could relax, however, he reckoned without Mansell, who was driving as if possessed. Patrese was no problem as the Ferrari breezed by into second place on the 22nd lap, and the *tifos*i was electrified by his menacing pursuit of the McLaren. By the 36th lap the two of them were nose-to-tail through *Tamburello* and as they exited the curve Mansell dived to the left of the McLaren, out of Berger's slipstream. But this was at the precise moment that Gerhard was pulling to the left to take his line for *Villeneuve*, and inadvertently he nudged Mansell on to the grass. The red car instantly rotated through a full 360 degrees before, incredibly, Nigel simply gathered it all up and carried on, losing only 3.1 seconds in the alarming incident!

Predictably, he ranted for a while about it afterwards, but Berger hadn't actually seen him, and in any case had been expecting an attack as they went into the braking area for *Tosa* rather than before. He simply hadn't appreciated just how quickly Mansell had taken the Ferrari through *Tamburello*...

"The first I saw of Nigel was when he was on the grass, with his nose level with my cockpit," he said afterwards. Some years later he would expand on his thoughts at that moment: "When I saw him go I thought, 'Good! That's the end of him!' but then he was right there again as if nothing had happened!"

Indeed, the Austrian would have little respite, for Mansell was attacking again within a few laps, but just as he seemed poised for another assault the Ferrari's V12 engine succumbed to the inevitable. It had been smoking throughout the race, and on the 39th lap it finally exploded, leaving Mansell to do a little exploding of his own the moment he found somebody to listen.

Berger really could relax now, as he led from Patrese and Nannini in the second Benetton, Alessandro having gone ahead of the other Ferrari when Prost made a fast stop to switch to the C compound Goodyears he should have used in the first place. It didn't happen often, but Alain really had got his set-up wrong this time because he was also running too much downforce, which deprived him of the straightline speed he needed to try and tackle the Benetton. Thanks to Mansell's earlier antics, he also had to contend with a sticking throttle after dirt had got into the slide mechanism.

Behind him, Piquet and Alesi had had a real set-to in the early laps, swapping sixth place on lap 18 at *Tosa* as the Brazilian went ahead. Then Jean elbowed his way back in front again at the same spot on lap 23, but this time the two cars touched and the Benetton was thrown into the air and landed hard, slightly skewing its suspension alignment. Alesi, meanwhile, had needed a set of fresh Pirellis after spinning, which meant that they were no longer running together.

Further back still, Martin Donnelly was making a very strong impression in what sadly would be an all too brief Formula One career, scything through the field in his relatively uncompetitive Lotus-Lamborghini so that in the closing stages, though his helmet visor was smothered with so much oil that he could barely see, he was able to chase team-mate Derek Warwick to the flag.

In 1983 Patrese had gained – and almost immediately lost – the lead on the 55th lap. This time, a relentless chase after Berger's fading McLaren took him into a position to challenge for first place by the 51st lap after the Austrian's Honda V10 had begun to lose its edge and his tyres their ultimate efficiency in the battle with Mansell. For the first time since that fateful day seven years earlier, Riccardo, who had recently celebrated his 36th birthday, looked set to win in his own backyard.

This race would be the embodiment of all that was good about the man who had been so vilified early in his Formula One career. In Brazil the previous year, Patrese had edged ahead of Graham Hill's longevity record of 176 Grand Prix starts, and as the perceptions of him changed he learned how to relax. He was no longer taking his work and its frustrations home with him, at times taxing his relationship with wife Suzi to extremes, and he was learning better how to roll with the punches. His steady maturation was one of the better aspects of that period of Formula One.

Riccardo loved testing, and his loyalty to Williams bordered on the fantastic, for he would never denigrate either car or team publicly, and the problems with reliability which affected the early stages of the development of the new Renault package no longer got him down as they might have done five years earlier. Williams, in particular Patrick Head, loved him, and he felt comfortable in an environment where his contribution was clearly valued highly. He had come close to the top of the mountain in Canada and Hungary the previous year, and at Imola, driving his 195th Grand Prix, Riccardo was ready for the challenge when the gods dealt the cards his way.

This time there was no sudden mistake as he overhauled the McLaren and headed home to an emotional win – his first in front of his home crowd. What made it better still was that this was the new Riccardo.

Back in the old days, at Arrows, Brabham and then Alfa Romeo and Brabham again, he had been misunderstood and had come across as an arrogant, aloof driver. But with the help of the Williams team, and in particular the job that public relations co-ordinator Ann Bradshaw did in persuading the British specialist press that he was a much maligned individual, Riccardo had emerged as one of the most popular stars of the day. Whereas the crowd had catcalled him and then jeered after his ignominious exit from the 1983 race, this time they cheered him to the echo as he led Berger across the line by 5.117 seconds; and so did the press, for the brigade in the press room was genuinely delighted for him.

"Well, the emotion was very big!" he admitted. "I always felt as if Imola was my home Grand Prix because it is very near to my home in Padova. I started driving in Imola, and I like very much the circuit. I know all the public is very much for Ferrari, but I feel at home. Also, is a race I missed in 1983...

"Winning this year the way I did it was fantastic, because I think I drove a good race and also because it was following last year's season where I tried very hard to win and sometimes was very close and missed the wins. I think I was repaid all the things that happened in the past, not just last year, but since 1983.

"I think it was the best win, and to win after seven years, after going through bad periods like I have had, to come back to the top, is not easy. Usually in Formula One when you go down and you are not a World Champion – World Champions always have credit – they always think they can replace you. If you are World Champion you have a very strong position. When you go down as I went, is difficult.

"I think my career has been in two periods; it was up to 1982/'83, down very badly in '84/'85, and then started again from '86 and to the period where I am now. I am pleased.

"You know, some people came to me and said you have a lot of bad luck in your career, and I say I don't think is a question of bad luck. I have good moments, bad moments, this is life. And anyway, I am quite happy with what I got from Formula One now.

"I always enjoyed what I did, my job, my work, because always I have tried to have this nice atmosphere around me, so even when things were bad there was always good morale, good spirit within the team. Because of that I always liked to stay in the ambience of Formula One.

"If you have bad moments and also there is no communication between members of the team, that is terrible. In effect, at the end of '85 a little bit of this came out with the Alfa Romeo team; there was not much communication, not much trust one side to another. I should say that the last part of the season was the worst, not because we were having bad moments technically, but very bad moments between persons. Fortunately, Bernie came again and said did I want to go back to Brabham, and gave me again the chance. Probably, if Bernie did not pick me out of the rubbish, it was the end of my career!"

And so the wheel came full-circle for the man whose apparent arrogance had worked against him in his early days, and who would be the subject of the witchhunt initiated against him by James Hunt following Ronnie Peterson's death at Monza in 1978. By 1990, Riccardo Patrese was no longer perceived as Formula One's *enfant terrible*, and had again been accepted into the eclectic fold. More than that, he now stood as one of its most popular protagonists and elder statesmen, a situation that secretly he probably found grimly ironic, yet which he clearly delighted in.

Riccardo Patrese, 1990 vintage, and Imola. It was a cocktail that pleased nearly everyone. If you had had to choose a combination of victors prior to the start of the season, you could scarcely have improved on that, because another triumph for Williams and the newly emergent Renault V10 engine struck what was generally seen as a welcome blow against the steamroller might of McLaren and Honda.

It was, in many ways, the happiest period in Riccardo's lengthy career, certainly far happier than his final season with Benetton in 1993 would ever be, yet he drew a fine distinction.

"I think, yes, I am quite happy," he said with the boyish smile so reminiscent of the Fifties actor John Cassavetes. "I've been happy many times, but now is much easier, because all the world says that I am a good person, that I'm driving well. I think I change a bit over the years. All the criticism I got in the past I don't think is completely wrong. Probably I was not expressing myself in the correct way. For sure I was different from what all the world described me as in the first part of my career. I was not like that, for sure, but I was not able to show to everybody that I was different to what they thought. Now I am able to show it because I am more mature, everything is going better, and because I'm more mature I'm able to speak more openly with people.

"I would not say that this is necessarily the happiest moment, because there have been many in the past, but let's say is the easiest, because everybody helps me. Everything is positive."

Nothing could have been more different from the Riccardo Patrese who had slunk from Imola at the end of the 1983 race than the man who stood beaming atop the podium this year. He had, he said, driven the last lap with tears in his eyes. The ghost, finally, had been exorcized.

RON PLACATES FERRARI

At times, Ron Dennis' face was Ferrari red in Imola following a gaffe in Interlagos when he had suggested to Italian journalists that there had been something underhand in the way in which Ferrari had invited his engineer, Steve Nichols, to leave McLaren and go and work on Alain Prost's car.

By Imola he had felt obliged to visit Maranello in early April for a capitulative meeting with Chairman Piero Fusaro and his deputy, Enzo Ferrari's second son Piero Lardi-Ferrari. A joint statement was then issued, which read: 'After a frank exchange of views, Mr Dennis reassured Mr Fusaro that his comments were never intended to suggest that Ferrari had acted improperly, or in a manner which was calculated to damage the spirit of fair play.'

This was a time when Ron was still very sensitive to the fact that Prost had left in the first place, let alone gone to Ferrari, and he was still feeling miffed that he had not been able to perform the miracle of getting Senna and Prost under sufficient control to work together. Failing to win has never come easily to him.

12
A fiasco for Ferrari

*"The internal crisis is something which is almost normal in Ferrari.
When we win there is a crisis of optimism; what we are going through at
the moment is even worse."* – Alain Prost

Ayrton Senna would make yet another little bit of history in 1991, and in
becoming the first man ever to win the first three races of the season, he
scored an easy triumph over team-mate Gerard Berger on a day when
their opposition simply fell apart.

At the beginning of the season Williams had introduced its brand new
car, the FW14, which had every sign not only of being highly competitive,
but of possessing the ability to dominate. Like Ferrari, it used a semi-
automatic transmission, but at this stage of the model's development its
reliability did not match its latent speed.

McLaren had a new Honda V12 engine to play with; the Honda
engineers, not to mention McLaren's, would all have been very happy to
stick with the successful V10 which had won them the titles in 1989 and
1990, but Soichiro Honda himself had dictated the V12, so V12 it was,
difficult packaging and all.

Ferrari, meanwhile, was persevering with its own V12 but, having
partnered the mercurial Jean Alesi with Alain Prost, the team was still
struggling to regain the momentum lost when Senna had taken Prost
out of the Japanese Grand Prix at Suzuka the previous October, almost
certainly costing the Prancing Horse its first World Championship since
1983.

Though the McLaren MP4/6 was less wieldy than the Williams FW14 or
the Ferrari 642, Senna took his customary pole position at Imola in 1m
21.877s, just ahead of Riccardo Patrese, who at that stage of his career
was making a habit of out-qualifying his new team leader Nigel Mansell,
much to the latter's chagrin. Riccardo recorded 1m 21.957s, with Prost
third on 1m 22.195s and Mansell fourth on 1m 22.366s. Berger shared
the third row with the Italian Stefano Modena, whose Tyrrell used the
now superseded Honda V10 engine, while Alesi was seventh fastest, just
ahead of another quick Italian, Gianni Morbidelli, in the Ferrari-engined

Minardi M191. His team-mate Pierluigi Martini, and Satoru Nakajima in the second Tyrrell, rounded out the top 10.

The *tifosi* had high hopes of their drivers, but as one Italian observer remarked wryly: "The difference between Senna and Prost is that they are both raging at their teams, but Ferrari isn't winning..." And, indeed, the red cars seemed to have lost the edge they had been honing all through 1990. Senna was confident of victory, but even he could not have foreseen just how relatively easy it was going to come.

It had been foully wet on the Saturday during second qualifying, and after a watery sun appeared on Sunday morning the sky darkened again and it rained at 1.30pm, half an hour before the start, and just as the cars were going on to the grid. It was the time for wet tyres and wet set-ups, but there were no extra acclimatization laps for the drivers.

From the grid they went round for the usual final warm-up lap prior to the green light, but Prost did not make it even that far. As he turned into the gentle right-hander that precedes the first *Rivazza*, the Ferrari slid from his control as it aquaplaned and then slithered down the hill on the wet grass before coming to rest backwards. Alain had stalled the V12 and couldn't restart it, and it gradually began to dawn on the stunned *tifosi* that its best runner was already history. And for Ferrari, worse was to come.

"I don't remember any particular reason for Alain going off," admitted his engineer at that time, the American Steve Nichols. "It was extremely wet. It sort of rained on the grid and they set off on their warm-up lap. But I don't think there was any particular reason. He was up the front and he just fell off. All you can say is that the people coming along afterwards had the benefit of his mistake.

"I'd have to say this about Prost; he was pretty damn good and he very rarely made mistakes. It's difficult to second-guess him on that one. It was one of the few mistakes he made in his career. You could say he made two mistakes then, really. He went off the road in the first place, and he didn't catch the engine, because even with the semi-automatic transmission then, we had a foot clutch. Probably Alain was so shocked at going off on the warm-up lap that he didn't even think of trying to catch the engine!

"It's very difficult to be critical. People make mistakes, and the conditions were atrocious. In addition to that, it rained on the grid, and you've got to think: 'What do we do now?' And you alter the set-up and off they go.

"My own personal attitude was that the guy does such a good job all of the time that you've got to allow him the odd mistake. I mean, we were very disappointed, and obviously others in the Ferrari camp took a less sympathetic view. They were extremely disappointed, inevitably, especially with what happened with Jean later on..." The *tifosi* were in no mood to sympathize with Prost, for all they could see was a pretty elementary driving error that had cost their man the race. Three laps later they were screaming themselves hoarse at Alesi, too, for much the same reason.

Ferrari's fiasco of a race soon unfolded. Patrese led off the line as Mansell's Williams lagged. The Briton had instantly dived for the gaping gap left by the absent Prost, only to find his semi-automatic transmission selecting him neutral rather than second gear. He fishtailed wildly and then almost stopped, leaving Alesi with a quick avoidance to make, and frustrating a following Martin Brundle. He had come speeding up from 18th on the grid in his Brabham-Yamaha and was right on Mansell's tail as they sped through the last corner to complete the lap, but then they misunderstood one another.

"I was right behind him and through the last chicane he slowed and went wide as if he was pulling into the pits," said Brundle. "Then all of a sudden he came across me and drove over the front of my car." As Brundle limped round for repairs, a furious Mansell became the second casualty among the leading runners.

Patrese continued to lead from Senna, Modena and Alesi, but then on lap three came the second awful moment for the *tifosi*. The Frenchman squeezed ahead of Modena on the outside on the run to *Tosa*, but the Ferrari began to snake badly as he braked hard for the hairpin, and as he ran wide and missed his apex the red car slithered inexorably towards, and into, the gravel bed on the outside. Jean gamely tried to extricate himself, revving the V12 to near maximum, but it was to no avail and he only succeeded in digging himself in further. It was an inglorious exit.

The *tifosi* were stunned as he trudged back to the pits, accepting their catcalls with resigned gestures that did nothing to alleviate his embarrassment. Within another lap the gates were jammed with angry, wet Italians leaving for home... It mattered little to them that Nelson Piquet had rotated his Benetton out of 12th place after only two laps, or that even Senna had almost come to grief in the difficult conditions. "I just held it," he revealed, "and then I was absolutely sure caution was the only way in the early stages."

At first Patrese had edged away from Senna, building a 6.3-second cushion after five laps, and the *tifosi* who remained began to prepare themselves for a repeat of his 1990 victory. But after 10 laps Senna had caught him, and the Brazilian overtook as the Williams hiccoughed and slowed. Something was clearly amiss, and when Riccardo pulled into the pits a faulty camshaft sensor was diagnosed. He did eight more sporadic laps, but then retired when his Renault RS3 quit altogether.

That left the McLarens an apparently straightforward run to the chequered flag in a notably dull race, though Berger was thanking the gods after slipping off the road at the same time as Prost had. Whereas

124

Alain had stalled, however, Gerhard was able to regain the track. He took third place from Modena on the lap that Piquet spun, then chased Senna home to finish a tad under two seconds behind.

Though that appeared to be 'situation normal' for McLaren, neither driver had had an easy run. At one point Senna had been seriously delayed by stupid driving from Modena on lap 30. As the McLaren driver attempted to lap the Tyrrell, Modena steadfastly held his line and blocked the Brazilian as he himself attempted to lap Thierry Boutsen's Ligier. Senna backed off and waited after the first chop at *Tosa* had pinched him over the kerb, but he was repelled again in his second try at *Rivazza*. It wasn't until two further laps had been completed that he outfumbled the Italian at *Tosa*.

Berger, meanwhile, had closed up during all this, but then had to cope with the return of a caliper fault that had made braking erratic in the morning warm-up, during which he had nevertheless been fastest. Like Senna, who had had a spell worrying about a blinking oil light, the Austrian would find that the problem rectified itself as the race progressed.

When Senna crossed the finish line he exorcized the ghost of Bill Vukovich from the World Championship. The wild Slavonian had won the Indianapolis 500 in both 1953 and 1954, and by doing so had deprived both Alberto Ascari and Juan-Manuel Fangio of the right to claim to have won the first three races of a year's World Championship. Both Ascari and Fangio won the first three European rounds in the respective seasons, but in those days Indy counted as an official round of the Championship, and was the second race of each year. In 1957, Fangio had also won the first three European races, but on that occasion Sam Hanks had triumphed at Indy, which was again the second round... It was all somewhat spurious, but now Ayrton became the first man officially to have won an opening hat-trick since the World Championship was inaugurated in 1950.

Despite his intransigent behaviour, Modena looked a reasonable bet for third place until his gearbox gave out after 41 laps, while a lengthy run in fourth place (which became third on Modena's demise) was interrupted for Roberto Moreno when the second Benetton began to lose gears; first of all second disappeared, then fifth. After a while, sixth gear went missing as well, and after several over-revs as a result, his Ford HB succumbed with six laps left.

That let JJ Lehto into third place, the Finn having pushed very hard behind the similarly Pirelli-shod Benetton with his Scuderia Italia Dallara-Judd. He finished one lap behind the McLarens, and said with a huge smile: "This was the best day of my life." It would also be the best result of his unfulfilled Formula One career, on the circuit where it would be all but destroyed three years later.

Further back, it was Belgian *v* Belgian, *mano a mano* for fifth place, as debutant Eric van de Poele and the experienced Boutsen fought in Martini's wake. In his first Grand Prix, van de Poele was driving the ungainly Lamborghini V12-engined Lambo 291, while Boutsen's Ligier JS35, which had been delayed by a brace of tyre stops, used a similar engine. Just as Boutsen was poised to snatch the position he dropped back with a cracked exhaust, and then, within sight of points at the first try, poor van de Poele suffered that old Imola disease: shortage of fuel. As he coasted to a halt the battling Lotus duo of Mika Hakkinen and Julian Bailey sped gratefully by for fifth and sixth places. For the Finn it was the start of something big; for the Briton, sadly, it was the zenith of his Grand Prix career. For Lotus, which had been reborn under the stewardship of Peter Collins and Peter Wright, it was a desperately needed fillip following the death after a fall the previous weekend of mechanic David Jacques.

For McLaren-Honda, meanwhile, it was yet another crushing success that, ultimately, would prove one of the bricks in the wall of Senna's third World Championship. But for Prost, whose parade lap spin had been the end of the beginning, it was also the beginning of the end with Ferrari. Some of the senior management, who had never taken to his way of trying to get rid of the team's seemingly ever-present inertia and intrigue, now had the bone they could keep gnawing away at.

Even before the race he had been outspoken about the team's management and its penchant for crisis. In an interview with the French press he had said: "In Ferrari, when things don't work, the guilty party has to be found, or excuses. So one day one person is blamed, another day it's somebody else. Today, for example, it's Steve Nichols, who is called into question because the chassis is not working. For me this is a scandal because it is not his fault at all. What is certain is that the choice to tackle the '91 season with the 642 was not made by Nichols or myself, but by the management.

"The first problem is that our testing went well over the winter; the second problem is that we did some of the testing with the 1990 aerodynamic set-up.

"In my opinion, the gap between McLaren and Williams and ourselves is due to our own problems. There are experienced people who know the problem. Then there are less experienced people who can also take decisions. The internal crisis is something which is almost normal in Ferrari. When we win there is a crisis of optimism; what we are going through at the moment is even worse.

"When there is a crisis of optimism everything stops. Nothing must be done – reliability must be bet-on, and this is going to win the Championship. That's what's happened during the inter-season. The problem is that here there are one or two people in the team who've got very little Formula One experience, so they think if a car is competitive at the end of a season, it should be kept for the beginning of the following season. That was true perhaps 10 years ago, but today things change so quickly from race to race that one cannot stand still."

And he had added one final barb, perhaps the most damaging.

"The structure at McLaren is much more efficient than ours. Ron Dennis has been a mechanic, knows Formula One, and has been in motorsport for a long time. He is a leader of men, a catalyst for energy. He is totally respected, and that's what's lacking here. If we had someone like him in our team, given our potential, we would be assured of being World Champion each year..."

Watching and listening to some of the Ferrari team at work that year, one was often tempted to remind them that, bar his own team-mate trying to intimidate him in Portugal, and old rival Senna physically shoving him off the road in Japan, Prost would have brought them the World Championship crown in 1990. Memories in Formula One are notoriously short, and if he ever had time off from his other professional duties, Prof Watkins could probably do a nice sideline in treating outbreaks of selective amnesia. Plenty of people within Ferrari wanted Alain Prost's head on a platter after his remarks, and with his own glaring error on that warm-up lap at Imola he had gone a long way towards presenting it. From then on it was only a matter of time. He was finally sacked ingloriously after the Japanese Grand Prix at the end of the year.

MICHELE'S LUCKY ESCAPE

With a Porsche contract in his pocket and a long-term deal to lease his team's name to wealthy Japanese industrialist Wataru Ohashi, Arrows owner Jack Oliver was in buoyant mood as the rechristened Footwork team unveiled its FA12 early in 1991 in readiness for testing prior to Imola. "I believe," said Jackie O happily, "that we may have pulled off the deal of the decade."

As events turned out, decayed might have been more apposite, for Porsche's bulky V12 engine would prove an unmitigated disaster. Alan Jenkins' new chassis was much better than its power unit, but even that had an unfortunate début when Michele Alboreto had a very nasty shunt in testing during the week that preceded the Grand Prix. The nose wing broke off just as he reached *Tamburello*.

"It was very well documented," said Jenkins. "Max Welti, who was looking after the Porsche programme at the time, managed to get hold of official film and we had it broken down frame by frame. The FA12 had a single-pillar nose wing, which worked well in the wind-tunnel, but though we had a series of load tests of our own we found that the wing used to get a little bit of a flutter. Our programme was a sort of mid-season thing because the car was introduced with the idea of racing it at Imola. The car ran in typically horrific cold weather for a day at Silverstone's South loop and then went off to Italy, and then it started going a fair amount quicker. And we also had the first signs of the serious oil cooling and circulation problems we would have with the engine. So it was a very disjointed test, and the accident finished it off, really.

"Basically, the car arrived across the kerbs and hit the wall at a very shallow angle, and then ran along the wall, sort of destroying itself. The first thing, obviously, was the cause of it, which was relatively straightforward to remedy. But it was similar to Berger's accident because we weren't sure whether Michele had run over a kerb prior to that, so we had to do a fair bit of looking around.

"But the car stood up to it pretty well, really. The accident lasted a long time, it went on forever. It was almost a true lateral impact. Certainly it was one where, if you take the new regulations introduced after Senna's accident, they would have helped. The photos show that Michele's body and head protruded a long way from the side of the car, and it was only a matter of inches from the wall. That's something that we've only recently got round to feeling not totally confident, but partly confident about; that we can address that problem without introducing another one.

"The other things that happened were all the typical ones. The problem with side impacts is where the wishbones end up. We had one go through the tub, but that's very difficult to do anything about. It went in and sliced underneath his thigh, missing him. It helps that today we have all moved the driver back, which pretty much guarantees that the thighs are going to be okay. Michele had stitches in his leg, but he was otherwise okay.

"He is remarkably together, Michele, in situations like that. Certainly his head remained pretty clear. He got out of the thing himself, and there was a picture of him standing next to it. That's the incredible thing! The last picture in the sequence is the most amazing one. There's this trail of destruction, and then there's the man looking at it!"

"I was knocked about a lot, but basically, apart from a couple of stitches in my leg, I just felt like I'd been beaten up," said Alboreto.

"One single accident is pretty straightforward," continued Jenkins, "but the difficult part is always a secondary impact, whose further effects are almost impossible to plan for. There was a front and a rear impact because it broke the gearbox and there was a gearbox oil fire. And, in the middle of the sequence, there is a big flash fire, which was that oil, not fuel.

"It's the classic thing for a designer, isn't it? We've all had the odd car destroyed, and certainly in those days I was quite close to Michele. That's the worst part of the business, really. Being on the edge of that sort of situation. That's half the reason why we people on the Technical Working Group get hot under the collar, really. I think everybody has their own concerns about safety for such reasons, but after Ayrton's accident it would become a joint concern."

13
The crying game

"I went back to the hotel that night and I was a very unhappy man. A seriously unhappy person." – Martin Brundle

Confidence is everything to the racing driver. It affects his attitude, his behaviour, his motivation – and, of course, his ultimate performance. Many things can boost it, and many can break it. It can be as solid as bricks and mortar, or as fragile as a mist at dawn. Like the actor or the surgeon, he needs to be at the very peak of his confidence to do the job properly.

Imola in 1992 was the story of Nigel Mansell's continuing confidence as he broke Ayrton Senna's record of four victories in the first four races of a season by winning his fifth. But it was also about the story of another sportsman's confidence as he plumbed the absolute depths of despair and stared complete failure and the end of his career in the face, before pulling himself together and using that peep into the abyss of destruction as a springboard to relaunch himself the following day.

As we drove to Fontanelice on the Thursday before the race we had more pressing matters on our minds, however, for we realized that other things were changing, too. Italy, once the country in which racing cars were driven with abandon across 1,000 miles of public road during the Mille Miglia epic, and where the excesses of fans might once have been forgiven simply because it was race week in any given town, was taking note of the rest of the world. On the main road from Imola to Fontanelice – the S610 that goes through Ponticelli and Borgo Tossignano – the *caribinieri* had set up radar traps to net those unwary enough to be speeding. There was something incongruous and hilarious about the sight of these men in their black and white uniforms, grasping their anything but amusing-looking sub-machine guns, while standing boldly alongside Fiat Pandas that didn't look big enough to house the men, let alone their impressive armoury. It was an unwelcome sign of the times, and thereafter we took to using the infinitely more picturesque – and safer – back road to the circuit each day.

By 1992, Williams had developed its active suspension concept to perfection, and in the FW14B Nigel Mansell finally had the equipment with which to snatch his overdue World Championship. Where Patrese had been able to out-qualify him for the first seven races of 1991 in the passive FW14, the active version was perfectly suited to Mansell's charging, brave style. It was a car that required less finesse than its predecessor, and responded better to brute force, to being slapped around a bit.

On that first day of qualifying Mansell was simply in a class of his own as he lapped the track in 1m 21.842s, a time that would remain sufficient for pole position. Only Senna got close that day, with a time of 1m 23.086s that would ultimately give him third place on the grid after Patrese had improved to 1m 22.895s the following day. Berger would be fourth in the second McLaren, while the third row of the grid would be fought out between the Benettons and the Ferraris.

While Michael Schumacher and Ivan Capelli got on quietly enough with their qualifying that day, though, Martin Brundle and Jean Alesi indulged in another episode of a feud that had been brewing for some time. In Brazil, for the opening race of the season, they had collided on the pit straight while fighting for third place, but their enmity went back a lot further than that.

"I think it really started back in 1989, when I was in the Brabham and he was in the Tyrrell," said Brundle reflectively. "We had a few run-ins. We're different people and we've got different driving styles. We're different characters completely, but we always seem to end up roughly in the same place on the track. But yes, it really started in 1992 when he was at Ferrari and I was at Benetton, and we had two cars of roughly the same performance.

"I caught him at the Brazilian Grand Prix and tried to pass him for third place, and we got into a huge Formula Ford-style weaving match down the pit straight. I just timed it such that I dived to the inside. What he was doing was outrageous, I know that. And it was all in front of the stewards and I'm surprised nothing happened.

"Anyway, it was after a pit stop and my car was significantly faster, and I ended up going down the inside of him. Then he promptly came left again and drove me straight into the wall." There were big tyre marks all down the Benetton's sidepods to testify to the contact.

"I slammed straight into the wall. I remember thinking 'Ooh, this is going to hurt!' and pulling my legs back, but the cars are so strong it took the impact in the front wing and corner. I lurched off the road at some alarming angle towards the pit wall, and it's a bit of a natural funnel, that bit of the track. You go uphill and the walls start coming in on you. It's quite a difficult braking area. But I never got that far. I arrived at the first corner, but going backwards and on three wheels.

"That was all a bit rude, really. It's unlike me, but I went straight to the stewards afterwards because I was so incensed at how unreasonable and dangerous it all was."

After a duff start to his Benetton career in South Africa, Brundle was also under pressure to perform within the team, which added to the scenario. "I was flying, and I wanted a good result, and I just felt he'd been unreasonable."

Peter Warr, the former Team Lotus manager, had been taken on by FISA as its permanent steward, and on the Friday prior to the race he had been outspoken about the governing body's intention to clamp down very hard on any driver who transgressed, for this was one of those frequent periods in which it seemed anxious to clean up driving standards. A book was going to be kept on each driver, and what Warr and company were going to do to those who got out of line didn't bear talking about, until the time for talking came and went and action was required. I taxed him about the situation afterwards, at the airport, and the gist of his response was that, er, Jean had one more chance, but would now be under close scrutiny. So much for authority...

In Mexico, Brundle had run very well until a water pump failed, and in the wet in Spain he had lost the clutch and eventually spun. When he arrived in Imola he was a man desperate for a smooth weekend and a good result. Equally, Alesi was in a position at Ferrari where he was expected to come up with the goods, and was also under tremendous pressure to lead the team in view of Capelli's disappointing performances, and to get the job done on Ferrari's home ground and in front of the hyper-critical *tifosi*. The clash that came that Friday afternoon had a kind of inevitability about it.

"Alesi felt that, coming out of the second *Rivazza*, I hadn't left him enough space as I was coming into the pits," said Brundle. "I felt that I had. I don't know, maybe I had, maybe I hadn't. It's a bit of a subjective issue, really. I knew he was there, and I felt I'd left him enough room to pass me between the second *Rivazza* and the chicane. He felt I'd interrupted his flow on his lap, in a Ferrari at Imola, remember. He does seem to have this approach that everybody else should be getting out of his way."

In fairness to Alesi, Brundle has a reputation as a hard boy to pass. Whatever, the two of them upset one another again. Besides the pressure of being a Ferrari driver in Imola, Alesi was distraught over the accident that had just befallen his close friend Nelson Piquet at Indianapolis, and he was generally not in the mood to be messed around. The twin-floored F92A wasn't performing well enough, either, and more than once Jean described it simply as "Shit." Towards the end of the session, when he was still only sixth fastest, he came upon the second Benetton.

Brundle continued: "I'd had a lousy morning when I lost fifth gear, and then I lost second in the afternoon, so I switched to the T-car and was on my first flier when I came across Andrea Chiesa in the first *Rivazza*. I tried to pass him, but had to back off. I think Jean must have thought that I did it deliberately to screw his lap, which I didn't."

Realizing that his own lap had gone, Alesi then pulled alongside the Benetton and the two feinted at one another, with Brundle moving over each time to avoid contact. Then, after Alesi had slowed again, Brundle repassed the Ferrari, before Jean overtook again and then put his right front wheel inside the Benetton's two left-hand wheels. Alesi then braked hard, and as the Benetton's left rear wheel rode over the Ferrari's right front, the yellow car was thrown into the air and spun to a halt. Later, Alesi warned Brundle: "If you try and block me, that's what I'll do..."

Three years later, Brundle said: "I was thrown quite high and did a 180-degree pirouette in the air, and I came down very, very hard. These things have little suspension travel, and I went straight through that and the floor of the car hit the ground where I was sitting and sent a shock up my spine.

"I was under a lot of pressure, and I think he was, too, but we were about to have a set-to at the entry end of the pit lane, with a lot of Italian marshals around us. It was like a mini stadium at the end of the Imola lap, if you remember, and there are the *tifosi*, waving their Ferrari flags and their *Tricolori* and all that sort of thing, and we're having a massive go at each other through our crash helmets. And then the helmets come off and it's getting seriously close to fisticuffs. I think the Italian marshals pulled us apart at that point... It was just two guys trying to do the same thing at the same time, with similar frustrations, I would imagine. That was a difficult day, and it screwed up my qualifying, but in the end we didn't get to scrapping, which was probably just as well as we'd have got a race ban, and it would have been very painful to the old bank account. But it had been brewing for some time..."

Alesi smiled, only a trifle sheepishly, later in the year when I reminded him of the incident. "I think, to be very clear, you 'ave to do things like that," he said. "Otherwise you are a traitor to yourself. I prefer that, rather than to go to someone else and say 'E is not good,' about somebody else. I prefer to be strong, to 'ave an explication at that moment, and then that's it. An explication, then closed. I prefer not to leave a thing open."

Some time later we touched on the theme again, after Jean had been critical of Coulthard's driving at Imola in 1995. "First of all I want to be clear on when I criticize somebody," said Jean. "For Brundle is different, because it is a very old story, and I don't criticize his way to do his job. It is just his comportment with me on the track. With Coulthard it was just the one time in Imola, and then it was argument closed. We spoke together and shook hands. I am not the kind of person who likes to criticize the other. I hate that, because everybody is doing a job, good and not good. I have one problem with one driver, is Martin Brundle. I don't know what it is, exactly. Is very old story..."

At the time Brundle was the very picture of a man in the depths of despair, and he told me: "It seems to be one setback after another. When your confidence is down your driving just doesn't flow. I can't get a rhythm. I know I can drive much better than this; I'm miles off what I can do, but I keep getting these little knocks. I should let the car do more of the work..."

It would only become apparent many years later just how shattered his confidence was that day, and how he dealt with the situation. His early years with Ken Tyrrell had clearly paid off when it came to concealing his true feelings.

Later that day a meeting took place in the Ferrari motorhome. "It was quite funny, really," Brundle said in 1995. "I'd never been in there before. It smelled just like the Ferrari I used to own, that was a very clear memory! That evocative smell of being in a Ferrari; obviously they use the same leather.

"Anyway, I think the idea of the meeting had been put together by Flavio Briatore and Cesare Fiorio, and it was quite funny because it was me and Michael, who had had a run-in somewhere with Alesi as well, and there was this sort of thing building between the Benetton drivers and Alesi. So there's me, Michael and Jean, Mr di Montezemolo on the phone from the factory, and Flav and Cesare. We needed to take the heat out of the situation, and it was the right thing to do. Ivan [Capelli] was making tea for some reason, I don't know why. But he was running around getting everyone a cuppa!

"It cleared the air a lot. It was exactly the right thing to do. Jean wasn't repentant, but none of us was. It was more all of us explaining our position. It took the steam out of it, those meetings always do. Jean was on the phone to Mr di Montezemolo at the factory, who came on halfway through the meeting. He felt it was better that the drivers sorted it out."

Somebody told Gerhard Berger about the handshake between Brundle and Alesi later on. It was just the sort of thing that amused the lanky Austrian, and he roared with laughter. "They do that?" he asked incredulously. "Then for sure they touch each other again in the first corner of the race, then!"

But they didn't. The animosity between Brundle and Alesi would remain, suppurating beneath the surface of Formula One for many years, but in that race at least they kept their distance. That day Martin Brundle exorcized his ghosts and drove like a demon, and it still registers as one of the few occasions on which a team-mate has actually outdriven Michael Schumacher.

Earlier that year I'd interviewed Martin for *Motor Sport* and he had been confident of challenging the young German. Later his story changed, for it was by then clear that Schumacher was a very special talent. Martin was the first to say it: "That kid is blessed with speed."

It might be argued that at that stage Schumacher had yet to have the Benetton team operating entirely to his whim, as it would in years to come, but that afternoon you could take nothing away from the Englishman's drive. However, it would be three years before the full story of how Martin had dragged himself back up became known.

"That Friday night was a disaster. This is my fifth race with Benetton and I've yet to score a finish. The meeting at Ferrari was Friday evening, and I was sort of verging on suicide at this moment. I'd been blown off yet again by Schumacher in qualifying and felt sure I was going to be dropped by Benetton. I'd signed for Benetton at Hockenheim in 1991, and from the moment I'd signed up until that Friday night in Imola there was speculation that I was going to be replaced by somebody. At that point it was Flavio and Tom [Walkinshaw] jockeying for position in the team, and I was very much seen as Tom's man. So I was under massive, massive pressure, both from the team and myself. And I was a very, very unhappy person.

"I went back to the hotel that night and I was a very unhappy man. A seriously unhappy person. But I have this mechanism in me, that enables this trip switch to go. It happened to me in 1983 with Senna as well, after he'd won the first nine Formula Three races. And at other times in my career. It happened to me in 1982, too, when I was under serious pressure in the BP Dave Price team because I had so little single-seater experience and had a very good Formula Three drive that I didn't have the experience to know what to do with. The trip switch went then and I put it on pole for the next five races and won two or three of them.

"I came back to Imola the next day and I, I think you'll find, that was the last time that Schumacher's team-mate actually beat him on the same day. But because it was a slower day I was two-tenths behind him on the grid. After the Saturday session I improved to sixth and, to his credit, he got straight out of his car, came to me in the back of the truck, and said 'Well done.' I'm not sure, but I don't think a team-mate has ever been in front of him from that day. I can't think of one..." Nobody would be, until circumstances went Johnny Herbert's way at Spa in 1995. The only other time had been when Nelson Piquet out-qualified Schumacher in Adelaide in 1991.

Brundle sometimes posted faster warm-up times than his team-mate, and in Canada and Spa that year he ran ahead of him in the races, but he was never again faster in qualifying. The previous day he had been well adrift with 1m 25.239s to Michael's 1m 23.701s, but that day he managed 1m 23.904s to Schumacher's 1m 24.177s. They lined up fifth and sixth on the grid, ahead of the Ferraris.

There was a false call when Karl Wendlinger stalled his March on the grid, but when the proper start finally came Brundle made a great getaway. Mansell led from pole with Patrese tucking in behind him, but as Berger blocked Schumacher, Brundle jumped past the second McLaren and only just thought better of trying to grab third place from Senna. "More than anything," he said, "I wanted a finish and I needed to be relatively conservative."

Senna, uncharacteristically, was also being cautious, though, which surprised Brundle enough to enable Berger to sneak back into fourth before the end of the lap, which ended Williams-Williams-McLaren-McLaren-Benetton-Benetton-Ferrari-Ferrari.

"I had a flying start," Brundle chuckled. "I was always demon at the start and I had Michael completely screwed in the head at the start of races. He was always busy looking for me and then running into Senna, or whomever, like at Magny-Cours that year – that was a classic!" [On that occasion Schumacher tangled on the first lap and retired early while Brundle went through to finish third.]

But things had started to look up for him at Imola. "I passed Michael going down to the first corner and I was running fourth behind Mansell, Patrese and Senna. Michael was right behind, and I could see he was all over the place, and eventually he just ran off the road at the second *Rivazza*, of all corners. And I went on to finish fourth after Gerhard hit Alesi because, as with my luck, nobody ever drops out... That was the turning point for me for the year."

The Williams duo was in a world of its own that afternoon, as it would so often be in 1992, and Mansell happily headed home to his record fifth win in five races and so create a little bit more history. And at the post-race interviews there was finally a hint of humility from the man who would be crowned Champion amid controversy later that season when he said: "This win is a tribute to reliability and I would like to dedicate it to the Canon Williams and Renault teams. All credit must go to the engineers associated with the team from Williams, Renault and Elf and all associated sponsors."

In the previous four races the Englishman had tended to play down the all too apparent superiority of his equipment, while playing up his own contribution, but this went some way to redressing the imbalance. During his race, he also admitted that the spectre of *Tamburello* had at times dominated his thoughts.

"I wanted to run my own race as I knew my tyres were marginal," he said, "and I was able to do this. But my biggest worry had been after Gerhard's accident with Alesi on lap 40, in case I got a puncture." No doubt team-mate Patrese's testing accident was uppermost in his mind at that point. "Then I had a fright at around 200mph when a marshal ran across on to the circuit..."

Further back, Senna was suffering from shoulder cramp and was so weary after finishing third that he stayed slumped in the McLaren's cockpit and missed the podium ceremony. Less than four seconds behind him was Brundle's Benetton, but not before the car had given Martin one fright when it lapsed momentarily on to five or six of its eight cylinders at *Tosa* close to the end. "I could have pushed Senna more, but I really needed a finish and I just didn't want to jeopardize that," he said.

It was a resurrection, but what had really triggered the trip switch on the Friday evening?

"Well, that night, when I got back to the hotel room I just sat down and let it all come out. I just sat down and cried. That's how people release tensions like that. It had really got to that, because I thought it was all over."

In a similar position a lot of drivers might have remained crushed and simply given up, but Brundle used his trip switch mechanism to fight back. "I just thought, 'Shit, I've got nothing to lose now.' And then you go out and just let your natural abilities come through. Instead of worrying about what might go wrong, which in some cases can actually trigger them going wrong, you just end up saying to hell with it.

"I felt as if I'd cleansed myself when I got to the circuit that Saturday morning, and I just drove beautifully the whole day, the rest of the weekend. And from that moment I was never out of the points except Canada, where the car failed. I never finished lower than fifth for the rest of the year, and I had five podiums."

He had been running well ahead of Schumacher in Canada, and by rights he should have won that race hands-down, but a faulty batch of differential bolts let him down. He never came so close to victory again, but after that day at Imola one Grand Prix triumph would have been just reward.

RICCARDO'S TESTING SHUNT AT TAMBURELLO

Once again the Williams team would go through the bruising experience of a shunt at *Tamburello*, and this time Riccardo Patrese would be the unlucky driver. It happened during a test session the week before the race, when he lost control of his FW14B at very high speed. This time the technology that the team had harnessed so successfully literally became its undoing.

"It was tyre-related," explained Patrick Head. "The tyre had got a puncture and Riccardo was not able to sense it because the active ride compensated for it. After that we had to build some sensing software in there which would then warn the driver with lights."

The chassis was a write-off, and Riccardo was concussed, but otherwise okay after another very lucky escape. After problems in qualifying on Friday he beat the chequered flag by a second as he ventured out in Mansell's spare car, and boosted his flagging confidence with a solid 1m 23.876s lap which placed him fifth overnight. The following day, though still bruised, the professional in Patrese beat the human being and he ignored his discomfort to record 1m 22.895s and join his partner Mansell on the front row. In the race he finished just under 10 seconds behind him after another typically stylish performance.

14
Damon lays a marker

"I don't think I used any tactics on you that I haven't seen you use before on other people." – Damon Hill to Ayrton Senna

The questions burned round the paddock in Imola on the Thursday prior to the 1993 San Marino Grand Prix as the producers and directors of the Formula One show stared at each other in panic at the thought that the star performer really might not turn up to take the spotlight on stage.

Where was Ayrton Senna? Was he coming? Would he really have the nerve to miss a Grand Prix? For a moment it was like the disappearance of Agatha Christie.

These were difficult times for the Brazilian. Superseded as World Champion the previous year by Nigel Mansell, he was now finding life less and less to his liking at McLaren. The writing had been on the wall for a couple of years, for he had constantly been urging McLaren to improve the behaviour of its chassis, whereas the team was constantly berating the Japanese engineers at Honda and demanding more and more horsepower in the battle with Williams and Renault.

Many paddock observers at that time believed that Honda and Senna had been McLaren's crutches, and that the Woking team's chassis were not any better than equal to the opposition, sometimes not even that. McLaren, naturally enough, strongly defended its technological competence. But now Honda had gone, and Ron Dennis and Senna found themselves in the unenviable position of being customers of Ford.

Though Dennis frequently spoke of a 'special relationship' between McLaren and Ford, the fact remained that Benetton was the works-assisted Ford team, and McLaren was buying its engines, even if it was undertaking a development programme of its own in conjunction with Cosworth Engineering. This all made for a very trying situation, for Senna was most definitely not a man used to second-best; he had not been, even at the beginning of his career, and he was certainly not going to settle for it now.

The situation was further complicated by the presence of Tom Walkinshaw as engineering director at Benetton, for Walkinshaw at that

138

time also had business dealings of a very tight nature with Ford. Though Dennis hated to admit it, Walkinshaw and Benetton had the whiphand.

To make matter worse for Senna, Alain Prost had joined Williams for 1993, taking over from Mansell as the Briton departed in high dudgeon for the American IndyCar series after failing to agree financial terms with his old team and making it clear that he wasn't interested in another partnership with the French champion. Prost had won the opening race in South Africa, but then Senna had won at home after Prost had spun in a rain shower, and had then dished out a terrific beating to Prost in the European Grand Prix at Donington on a surface that kept changing from wet to dry and back again.

But none of this was enough to placate Senna, who knew that, all things being equal on a dry road, even he wasn't going to get anywhere near either Prost's Williams, or that of the increasingly competitive new boy, Damon Hill. The latter, the son of late World Champion Graham Hill, had driven in two Grands Prix for Brabham the previous year, and had now risen from test driver at Williams to partner Prost in the best team in the business. As we shall see, he was also beginning to establish a reputation as a very cool, very quick customer who was not going to be cowed by running wheel-to-wheel with famous names.

At the very least, Senna was bent on getting parity of equipment with Benetton, for whom the emergent new star Michael Schumacher was looking increasingly strong. Of all his rivals, Senna knew even then that the German would be the most trouble in the future.

Senna and Dennis were playing an outwardly fraught poker game over money, and Ayrton had then gone back home to Brazil to let Ron stew awhile. It would later transpire that some of their apparent differences were mere play acting, to get others to do what they wanted.

Ostensibly, Senna was competing on a race-by-race basis since the two could not agree terms for his remuneration that year. Dennis had gone as high as he would go, and Senna was not prepared to back down, especially in the 'reduced' circumstances. Others were going to have to make up the shortfall in his salary demands. Honda's withdrawal had hit Ayrton very hard, and in retrospect, though it was no fault of Honda's, it set in motion the events that were to take him to his death a year later.

The general understanding at the time was that Senna might well pick and choose which races he would do, based on where he thought the Ford-engined McLaren package would be most competitive. Those events he would not do would be handled by the impressive Finn, Mika Hakkinen, who had moved from Lotus, but was not actually able to race for McLaren because Dennis had already agreed terms with the American IndyCar Champion, Michael Andretti, the son of former World Champion Mario. The belief in some quarters was that Senna did not plan to do the Imola race because of the premium the circuit at that time placed on sheer horsepower.

That Thursday, it really did seem that he might not be turning up, and various stories did the rounds. One of the more credible was that he had been out on the town with friends back home on the Wednesday night, getting back to his flat in the very early hours of the morning after some serious partying. This was quite clearly not the behaviour of a man who intended to participate at a Grand Prix in two days' time.

He wasn't coming, said the grapevine. He was on his way, in mid-air. He had landed in Italy. Every eventuality was covered by the rumours, which were developed and embellished in a way that only Italian journalists can achieve. Eventually he did arrive in time to practice on Friday morning, having taken the red-eye flight from Sao Paolo, but it was quite apparent that he was prepared to take the cold war with Ford to the absolute limit of brinkmanship.

He did not look well when he climbed aboard his car, having turned up at the circuit with literally only 15 minutes to go before the start of free practice, and his driving was erratic. This was partly because of a characteristic of McLaren's active suspension over bumps and kerbs, and partly because, like Fangio after his trip from Ireland to Monza back in 1952, he was not in the best condition to handle the car. He made several mistakes, including backing the McLaren into the pit wall after a spin. He was also in a foul mood.

There is a tendency to look back after apocalyptic events and to perceive everything that preceded them as innocent and free of concern. Formula One could never be described in such a way, but at this period it was free of the foreboding that would follow the 1994 race. This was the F1 we all knew or had come to know then, full of politics to give us something to write about, but comfortable. Nothing unexpected was happening. This kind of infighting was commonplace, however semantic it might be. Formula One was as bad as it ever was in some respects, but this would be the last year for a long time in which it would go about its business without that nagging shadow in the back of its mind, that dark recollection that never goes away for long.

This was the backdrop against which qualifying proceeded, and Senna's worst fears were realized as Prost took pole position, with Hill as company on the front row, while Schumacher was third ahead of his McLaren. Senna might have smiled as the rain predicted for Sunday arrived shortly before the start, for he knew from Donington just what he could do with the McLaren.

But it was Hill who grabbed the initiative as Prost lagged again with a baulky clutch (something he would complain about on the Williams for some time until a modification cured the problem), with Senna pushing ahead of Schumacher and then snatching second place from his old rival. Hill slid over the kerbs at *Acque Minerali*, but kept ahead of the Brazilian as they completed the lap.

Already, both Mark Blundell in a Ligier and Riccardo Patrese, in his last Grand Prix at Imola, had gone. The Briton had crashed at *Tamburello*, probably after contact from behind, while the Italian veteran's Benetton was nudged from behind at *Tosa*.

The first six laps were electrifying for the spectators, and terrifying for Prost as Senna weaved and dived all over the road to keep the Williams at bay. It was a stunning display of ruthless driving that Senna would only surpass later that year in the opening laps of the British Grand Prix, and his armoury of tactics were only ever brought to bear in such an unflinching manner against Prost. The Frenchman stoically applied himself to the job, and at *Tosa* that lap he finally outsmarted Ayrton and pulled away, no doubt breathing easily at last.

Hill, meanwhile, was leading comfortably, but the track was drying and slick tyres would soon be needed. As Senna and then Prost came in for them, Hill stayed out, aware that he had pitted too soon as conditions changed at Donington. This time, however, the earlier stop was the better policy. As he rejoined the race after his stop on lap 11 he found that Senna, who had beaten Prost out of the pits, was right on his tail again. Prost was there, too, preparing to go back into battle with his arch-enemy. As they sped towards *Tosa* the situation was complicated further by a glut of backmarkers, and in a wholesale game of nip and tuck they emerged with Prost having vaulted by both Senna and his team-mate by taking a wider entry line and finding more grip on the exit as a result. He now had a lead he would hold to the flag.

That left Hill to chase Senna, who had also nipped by him in the drama at *Tosa*; for a driver in only his sixth Grand Prix that was no mean challenge. Shortly after that, on lap 17, Hill had a huge fright as rookie Rubens Barrichello (the other star of Donington) spun his Jordan right in front of the Williams on the exit to *Tosa* during a heated battle with the underrated Lotus driver Alessandro Zanardi.

"His car was broadside and I was aiming straight for it," he said. "I was literally about a foot away when it spun just a little bit further and we missed each other... well, I just don't know how we avoided a collision. It was pretty close! I thought I'd had it."

Four laps later Hill's race was over. Going down to *Tosa* he got caught out when the brake pedal travel increased suddenly as he was slowing after getting a tow in Zanardi's slipstream. The Williams slid into the gravel trap, out of the race, leaving Hill to comment: "I was maybe a bit later on the brakes, and I was going in faster than ever because of the tow from Zanardi, but when I hit the brakes the pedal went to the floor." He reflected for a moment, and then added: "Perhaps that's a slight exaggeration, but when you need to go suddenly from 200mph to about 80 in under three seconds then, believe me, that's the way it feels."

Williams blamed a pad knock-off problem, Patrick Head adding: "The other factor is that Damon has enormous feet. Thus for him it is always very important that the brake pedal is in a particular position when he wants to apply the brakes. He brakes later than Alain, who rolls into a corner. But you still have to use the same amount of retardation. It's just that Damon brakes in fractionally less time. That means all that heat has to be dissipated in a fraction less time. And I think Damon was on a bit of damp track to pass Zanardi and that, like any racing driver, he was leaving his braking to the last moment. And the pedal was not quite where he wanted it to be."

Damon's race was over, but his part in the day's proceedings was not quite finished...

Senna held second place until the 43rd lap, when an electronic problem again blighted his McLaren on the run to *Tosa*. That grabbed his attention since it affected the entire handing and balance, and after he had scrabbled round the hairpin the car died altogether after *Acque Minerali*.

Ten laps later Prost nearly came to grief when his throttle stuck open momentarily going to *Tosa*, the corner where most of the action seemed to take place this year. He declutched and braked very hard and managed to get round, and thereafter he nursed his car to the finish.

Behind him, Schumacher brought the Benetton home second after an initial tussle with Gerhard Berger's Ferrari. This year the red cars were troublesome and uncompetitive, for this was a time when the Italian team was in the throes of some very serious reorganization, a time when its performances on track were reminiscent of BRM's at its worst.

Ferrari was struggling to hone its active suspension, while John Barnard sought to instil some engineering discipline into the team following his return to it; this time there would be nothing for the *tifosi* to cheer as the Austrian retired with gearbox failure after only eight laps, and Jean Alesi lost his clutch after 40 laps of sparkless racing. Third place thus fell to Martin Brundle in the Ligier, ahead of JJ Lehto's Sauber-Mercedes, Philippe Alliot's Larrousse-Lamborghini and Fabrizio Barbazza, who delighted Giancarlo Minardi by taking a point for sixth place.

It was a timely fillip for Brundle, who never quite understood – along with most of the British press – why he had been rejected by both Benetton and Williams during the winter of 1992.

"I got some justice for finishing only fourth in 1992, because I did make the podium this time," he smiled. "I went for dry settings in a wet race, and drove a stormer. Michael was second, and I remember him saying to me on the podium: 'Welcome back!', which was nice. That was another nice memory for me of Imola."

For Hill, that year's race brought another kind of recollection, for no sooner had the race finished than he was summoned to the McLaren motorhome for a meeting with Senna. The Brazilian had certainly taken on board the growing challenge from the Englishman, who had now run in the top three at stages in each of his four races for Williams, and had finished second in Brazil and again at Donington.

Hill had led Senna in Brazil, and again in Imola, and the former Champion was now distressed at what he believed to be unsporting tactics that Hill had employed to keep him back in the race from which they had both just retired. When he had seen Senna in his mirrors crawling all over the back of the Williams, Hill had said to himself: 'I'm not letting him through like I did at Donington' and later he admitted: "I had a good old time blocking him horribly." But that was only on that first lap in the scramble through *Tamburello* and *Tosa*. After that he had been able to pull away slightly.

Later, his defence of the lead after the first pit stops had been robust but fair, and in any case it hadn't lasted long. But Senna was still humming about it. When Hill arrived he was treated to a dressing down designed to belittle and humble him, and no doubt to intimidate him the next time he saw the yellow helmet in his mirrors.

Hill, however, is not susceptible to such tactics. He listened politely as Senna had his say, warning him never, ever to weave in front of him again. Not in front of Him!

Damon, who to his credit never spoke about the incident unless asked first, smiled faintly as he related the tale. "I just told him that I didn't think I had done anything to him that I hadn't seen him do in his career," he said. "There wasn't much he could say after that."

His very coolness made a big impression on Senna, who surely made a mental note about the tall Englishman with the bushy eyebrows and the penetrating dark eyes. It mattered not to Damon that at the end of the year they became team-mates at Williams, and though the prospect of partnering a man with a reputation for destroying team-mates cannot have been too enticing, he hid his feelings well. This, after all, was the driver who, when asked how he expected Senna to deal with him in 1994, had replied with an easy smile: "What do you think he's going to do? Put me in a Vulcan Mind Grip or something?" Sadly, we were all denied the chance to really see how they would have got on together.

The 1993 San Marino Grand Prix was to give Alain Prost his 46th victory and his third at the Imola circuit, and at the end of the season he would be crowned World Champion for the fourth, and final, time. But by Estoril in September he knew that his worst fears had been realized.

Despite knowing full well how Prost felt about the prospect of being teamed again with Senna, Frank Williams simply could not help himself and had come to an agreement with the Brazilian for 1994, whether it meant Prost would quit or not. The manner in which Prost had won his

1993 races, Imola among them, had simply made Senna all the more determined to get himself into the Williams chassis and sitting in front of the Renault V10.

In the long-running feud between the two of them it seemed that once again Senna had won. But as events were so sadly to reveal, it would prove a pyrrhic victory.

SENNA STYMIED

The week before Imola, Ayrton Senna had actually tested a McLaren MP4/8 equipped with the more powerful Series VII version of the Ford HB V8 that he so coveted. And when Ron Dennis had finally persuaded him to fly to Imola, the carrot was the brace of Series VIIs that were in the hold of the McLaren transporter, which Dennis had persuaded Cosworth to release. But even while Senna was airborne, a Cosworth employee had thought to double-check with Ford, which had instantly vetoed McLaren's plan to run them once Tom Walkinshaw had found out about it.

Wearing his Ford hat, the brawny Scot was prepared to let McLaren race the engines, even at the expense of Benetton's established preferential contract, which guaranteed it exclusivity of the latest equipment, but only provided that Dennis signed an agreement with Ford for 1994. Since Dennis at that time entertained serious hopes of snatching away Ligier's Renault engines for the following season, he was clearly not prepared to do that.

Walkinshaw had seen the situation coming long before it finally reached this climax. "This is exactly what I told Ford would happen back at the end of last year," he revealed. "I said that Senna would be sitting on the pit wall at Donington refusing to race unless he had the same engines. Well, I wrong; I was a race out."

A spokesman for McLaren said rather ingenuously: "I think coming late was Ayrton's different perception of how to put pressure on Ford. McLaren did not think that was appropriate, and we were able to convince him to turn up. We pointed out to him that it might look as if Benetton was winning the psychological war."

Whatever, when Senna found out that his trip had been in vain, he was livid.

15
Under the eyes of the world

"It's one of those things where you have to say: 'What level of danger is considered acceptable at any one time?' It's a moving target."
– Patrick Head

For a long time the fate of the 1995 San Marino Grand Prix hung in the balance, see-sawing between the need to carry out massive changes, and the political problems that raged behind the scenes. The organizers had attempted to buy the land to the outside of the track by *Tamburello* and *Villeneuve*, to facilitate modifications, but had been unsuccessful. Like the organizers at Monza, they had also run into trouble with vocal environmentalists when they disclosed that they would have to cut down trees on the inside of *Tamburello* in order to make the necessary changes to its trajectory.

The season had already started before final confirmation of the race came through, and on April 19, after the expenditure of some £5 million, the heavily revised *Autodromo Enzo e Dino Ferrari* was finally inaugurated, in the presence of the Bishop of Imola and other civic dignitaries and representatives of the military and the police.

Franco Lini had no time for any of the delays. "In the last year it was the bloody ecologists, the environmentalists. Oh! It is hypocrisy! Just like at Monza! I see the hypocrisy in all these political things and I just say, 'Stop! We are really tired.'"

It had been a prolonged battle and, like the best of them, victory had not come easily. The environmentalists had been overcome, and in separate deals the future of the San Marino Grand Prix had been secured until the year 2001, but at a price.

Imola's holding company, Sagis, had been obliged to sell the rights to advertising, entertainment, hotel rooms and catering within the track to FIA vice president of marketing Bernie Ecclestone, via his FOCA enterprise. It remained to be seen beyond that what influence it had on Imola as Fiat sought to recoup its significant investment in Mugello, which is not far away to the south-west, between Florence and Bologna.

"It is another story," insisted Lini. "Fiat has put a lot of money into

Mugello, after transferring the track to Ferrari, but I do not see it being a threat to Imola. That would be very unpopular. The Italian public opinion would not really accept that."

When the circus finally moved into town it was a very different Formula One troupe. In the end, not one driver had voluntarily quit the sport in the aftermath of the tragedies of 1994, but there was not a man among them who had not done an awful lot of soul-searching before taking the decision to continue. And the Grand Prix Drivers' Association was again a living body, with a vibrant voice and a genuine concern in safety matters. Death had united them. Some of the younger men had grown up in a hurry. Others had aged visibly. Though they might not talk about it, none had been left untouched in some way.

Everybody immediately began to take stock of the changes made to the track. Now *Tamburello* no longer curved forever to the left. Like the big sweeper at Interlagos, the flat-out bend had been consigned to the history books. Instead, there was a sharper turn to the left, to the inside of the old corner, followed by a right-hander that led back to another left, which rejoined the old track. It was slower and safer, with greater run-off area.

Now the track no longer ran flat-out down to *Tosa*, either, for instead of arcing gently right through Gilles' corner it now bore to the left, before a sharp right turn took the cars back to the old road on the approach to the hairpin. Again it was slower, and again it was safer, with greater run-off.

The best change concerned *Acque Minerali*, which had reverted to a double right-hand corner and was at last rid of its chicanery, while the *Rivazza* had been shortened, again to provide greater run-off area. The *Variante Bassa* had also been smoothed-out, to avoid the risk of a repeat of Barrichello's shunt. There was no shortage of opinion on the success or otherwise of the modifications.

"We all know why the changes had to be made," said Michael Schumacher. "We could not keep going flat-out through *Tamburello*. But we would have liked after the new *Tamburello* to have gone straight down to *Tosa*, avoiding the right-hand kink where Ratzenberger crashed. But the organizers could not buy the land there, and they could not keep the old layout because there wasn't sufficient run-off area, so they had to do what they did.

"I agree with those who say that it spoiled the flow of the track, but it's still Imola, and maybe they can buy more land in the future to change it again..." (Subsequently, agreement was reached with the owner and that particular parcel of land has been acquired by the Municipality, but whether any further use is made of it remains to be seen.)

Martin Brundle said he liked the changes. "I have always enjoyed Imola, and I still do, even though this time I'm not racing. I liked the changes when I tested there recently. Some of them have been very necessary; the two chicanes they've put in, together with the Abbey chicane at Silverstone, are the three best chicanes I've ever seen. If you put a chicane in, you won't do better than they have done there. And the new *Acque Minerali* works very well. Much better. But I'm really sad they tightened the second *Rivazza*.

"I don't care which driver you are talking about, we were all scared witless going through the old *Tamburello*. We just knew... It had absolutely nothing to do with your ability. It was very hard for the car in the dry, and nothing for the driver. In the wet you had to be careful to be flat through there, which was even more terrifying. But in the dry there was no driver skill whatsoever in going round *Tamburello*. Like all of these corners, in your mind's eye you think of a corner like *Tamburello* as easy flat, as a curve, but then you walk down and see it and look at the wall curving round, and you realize that it is a corner, a very long corner that turns through a lot of degrees, and you just always knew that the laws of physics were going to take you into that wall. And we had so many guys in there – Berger, Piquet, Patrese, Alboreto – having huge ones in there, that you knew that one day...

"I think that's the crying shame of 1994. That's what generated the drivers to get back together. To a certain extent, part of what drove us to have our meeting in Monaco, other than the tragedies, was the guilt feeling, that we all knew the situation about *Tamburello* – and one or two other corners in the world – and we tucked them to the back of our minds and hadn't done anything about them.

"It's very easy to say – I've seen some words where key people have said – 'Well, the teams always tested there, the drivers haven't said anything.' Which I think to a certain extent is relevant, but I don't believe that is altogether fair. It's that macho thing. You don't come in and tell your race team: 'Christ, I'm scared through *Tamburello*.' They'd look at you, look at each other, and think: 'Maybe we need a different driver.' People don't understand.

"It was interesting to see one of Frank Williams' comments the other day when he had a go in Renault's Espace that's fitted with the V10 Formula One engine, where you're going at half the speed through all the corners that an F1 car does. He said: 'Hey, I now know what my drivers are talking about, and everywhere I looked I realized there was a huge accident waiting if anything failed.'"

Brundle himself, a prime mover in the GPDA after the Imola tragedies, had found it wearisome and damaging for his morale and confidence to keep trudging round the circuits of the world on safety missions, and said: "It doesn't do you any good mentally after a bit to keep looking at all the places where you can have an accident."

That is just another part of the motorsport jigsaw that many people, outside of the drivers, had to learn about for the first time. Ignoring potential risks is every bit as important a part as calculating them. It's the nature of the game, however bland, misguided or cruel it might seem.

"We all accept it's dangerous," said Brundle, one of the most down-to-earth and articulate of drivers. "I think we all accept that you can break a leg, or you could die, otherwise you're burying your head in the sand if you're a Grand Prix driver or a racing car driver, or a downhill skier or whatever, if you think that it won't happen to me. I have come fully to terms with the fact that I may well die in a racing car. I've got a young family and all that sort of thing, but what I do, I am a racing driver. What you ask for is a reasonable chance to survive, and you didn't have that in corners like *Tamburello*. Your destiny was not in your own control."

Tamburello, and corners like it, were the sort of places professional racing drivers coped with when they were competing, but which could trouble the more imaginative in those hours at dawn before sleep comes.

"You always knew that if you thumped your front wings in *Acque Minerali*, for example," Brundle continued, "you'd better be thinking about calling into the pits, which was the sensible thing to do, before the next time you went through *Tamburello*. It wasn't a corner, but a kink in the road. If something broke you were dead, and that wasn't a legitimate risk. Whereas a corner like *Eau Rouge* at Spa, which we all love, demands input from the driver, and you can accept the risk on that sort of corner.

"At the same time you've got to have respect for Senna and what he achieved, and the guy that he was. And if they hadn't changed *Tamburello* I think it would have been a disgrace."

Another man who was delighted to see Formula One return to Imola was Ecclestone, and not just because of his deal with Sagis. "It's a very, very good venue. It's the closest we get to a city, isn't it? So it's convenient for everything."

Ecclestone is no stranger to death on the racetrack, for in his time he has seen many drivers killed, some of them his close friends, such as Stuart Lewis-Evans, Jochen Rindt and Carlos Pace. But he is a realist, and his reputation as a cold-hearted organizer of men, and one to whom the emotional side of the sport means nothing, takes something of a dent with his comments. Though his words sometimes have a directness that does not sit well with those who like to hide harsh reality behind a protective veneer, his points are nonetheless valid and well argued.

"Poor Senna; he could have had another hundred accidents like that one and walked away from the whole hundred. The chances are thousands to one against that ever happening, the actual thing that killed him. I won't discuss what caused the accident, but actually what caused his death was the suspension component. First of all it had to be broken off in a jagged way to act like a bloody knife. The chances of that happening were slim to none. And then it coming back in that exact position, where it wouldn't have glanced off his helmet, was also thousands to one, so the chances are slim. That's how it is. Ninety five percent of the people who were there had never been at a race where somebody had been killed.

"Ratzenberger got killed the day before and few people even thought about it. I had to go to the drivers' briefing and say: 'Do you think we ought to just be quiet for a minute or two because of what happened yesterday?' Some of them were laughing and joking, as if they'd hardly thought of it. So one minute's silence, then everyone went on. It didn't seem to affect anybody."

It is, perhaps, like the portrait Tom Wolfe depicted in his book *The Right Stuff*, about American test pilots and astronauts in the Fifties and Sixties; it wasn't that some drivers were being callous in concealing whatever emotions they felt, for some most certainly felt very deeply about Roland. But believing that the other guy had made a mistake was a self-protective shield that some used to convince themselves that it couldn't happen to them. Yet when it did with Senna, later that day, they were thrown into the sort of turmoil that had followed Jim Clark's death, when Chris Amon had spoken for all of his fellows with the remark: "We all felt that if it could happen to Jimmy, what chance did the rest of us have?"

"In this case it was Senna," continued Ecclestone. "If he had been killed like Roland, where it hadn't been seen on television, and he had been whipped to hospital, it wouldn't have created such a terrific impact. It would have created one, obviously, but it was the fact that for an hour people were saying: 'What's happened to him? Is he going to make it?' It was a public death. Like crucifying Jesus Christ on television.

"Had it been anyone but the two leaders, you wouldn't have picked it up [the accident] on TV. If it hadn't have been Senna it would have been Schmogel, and he would have been in 15th place. He'd have had his accident and it wouldn't have been seen, if you follow me."

In the immediate aftermath of the tragedies, Ecclestone was frequently portrayed as a man without heart, as an emotionless autocrat who had callously eaten an apple while off-handedly telling Senna's brother Leonardo of his death. He was crucified by the Brazilian press and specifically banned from attending the funeral by the Senna family. It was alleged that he knew Senna was dead by the side of the track, yet chose to keep up a charade. But Gerhard Berger has confirmed that when he saw Senna in the Maggiore Hospital he was still being kept alive on a life support machine.

In an exclusive interview with Nigel Roebuck in *Autosport* in July 1995, Ecclestone said: "He was dead, clinically, but he was alive. What was I going to do? As far as stopping the race was concerned, it had absolutely nothing to do with me. And, anyway, why should the race have been stopped? It wasn't going to bring the guy back. We don't stop flying every time there's a plane crash, do we?"

As Roebuck concluded, such sentiments seem hard-nosed, chilling even, when expressed in such a way, but Ecclestone's willingness to talk, unprompted, about 1994 is a telling sign, not of guilt, but of the warmth of his regard for Senna.

Like the rest of us, Bernie was glad to be back at the track he had first raced on in 1956. "I've always thought it was a lovely circuit. I've always liked Imola," he admitted. "I like the atmosphere and I like the people, because I was involved from the first day and the people were very close to me and we've been working with them. They were always very warm to me, and as far as I'm concerned it was a good atmosphere. I liked Imola and I liked to go back there. I would have been really, really upset if we hadn't. Everybody there, from the mayor down to the marshals, they're all enthusiasts, they all love their racing, and they all love racing."

One of those for whom a return to Imola could have been the hardest was Sid Watkins, for he more than any other had been right on the scene and had taken in the full horror of all three accidents during that black weekend in 1994. And hardened professional though he is, he had also had to go through the motions with Senna of doing what he could for a man for whom he had immense admiration and for whom he felt strong friendship. It was Prof who had arranged for Ayrton to visit Loretto School, on the Scottish border; Senna was fascinated by Jim Clark, who had been educated there, and he had addressed the boys and answered their questions. And it was Prof who used to stay with the hacks at Rosa's, in Fontanelice, for many years until other considerations obliged him to relocate a little closer to the circuit.

"I've always liked Imola, I've always liked the atmosphere there," he said. "The organization are decent people. The crowd are a much better behaved crowd than at Monza, and I've always enjoyed going there.

"The problem with the dreaded *Tamburello* is that we had so many shunts there and people walked away. There was Piquet, Patrese did it in practice, Alboreto did it, Berger did it. Years before that, Scheckter did it a bit further on, and so did Gilles when he had that bit of double vision for a few hours. It's extraordinary, we've had probably 10 accidents there, if you count them up. But it has to be remembered, too, that Balestre had a meeting with Senna, Prost and some others about that corner, and it was agreed to keep it...

"I was pleased to go back; I tried not to look at the bit of circuit where I'd been the year before. Fortunately, it had changed so much, and I think that helped a bit..."

Harvey Postlethwaite spoke for those who were disappointed with the solutions at *Tamburello* and *Villeneuve*, when he said: "It's a pity, isn't it, because they've fucked the place up. It's shitty now, frankly. I mean, you look at it now on the telemetry, and it's awful. It's just a series of... eight corners, all at the same speed! Crap!" But he paused and laughed ruefully as he added: "But it was good to go back!" Certainly, it was a long, long way from the track that Castellotti, Perdisa and Maglioli had raced on 41 years earlier.

On the subject of the new breed of cars, which had dramatic new safety requirements, reduced downforce, smaller fuel tanks and less powerful 3-litre engines, Footwork designer Alan Jenkins expressed the view: "Everybody's tried to do it as carefully as possible, but there's been a lot of shooting from the hip from other quarters, which makes you worry, because you could just as easily make the wrong step." There was general belief, however, that with the help of a working group of leading designers, the FIA had come up with an excellent compromise that held great promise.

The world's press descended *en masse* on Imola that weekend, the little town and its race track yet again bearing the focus of global attention. Daily newspapers in London had sent not just their regular reporters, but droves of 'colour' feature writers, almost in the expectation of history repeating itself.

There was another factor that drew publicity like a magnet, however, and that was the scheduled return of an old Italian favourite, Nigel Mansell, *Il Leone*. Having been dumped by Williams in favour of the young Scottish driver David Coulthard, Mansell and Ron Dennis had undergone a marriage of convenience at McLaren, but the honeymoon had been interrupted not only by the poor initial testing performance of the new car, but also by Mansell's inability to fit comfortably into it.

The design had been finalized before he had agreed his deal, and when it came to it he simply didn't have enough room in the cockpit of a car designed more with drivers of Mika Hakkinen's or Coulthard's size in mind, for had Williams opted for Mansell, the Scot would have gone down the road to Woking for a drive. Mansell had thus missed the two opening races while McLaren built him a modified chassis, but now he was finally scheduled to start his season.

Once again, and for a mixture of right and wrong reasons, motor racing was big news, and what we all saw was a triumph for the sport.

It was wet when race day dawned, and Alesi in particular thrilled the fans with some serious sideways motoring during the morning warm-up that not only encapsulated the character of the man, but endorsed just what a finely balanced chassis John Barnard had produced for Ferrari. The *tifosi* had genuine hopes, either for a maiden victory for the volatile Frenchman, or another for trusty team-mate Gerhard Berger, after they had qualified fifth and second respectively. The red cars had shown speed in both previous races, in Brazil and Argentina, and though Schumacher appeared to have taken over the mantle of Senna by putting the Benetton-Renault on pole, the Williams-Renaults of David Coulthard and Damon Hill were also in the 1m 27s bracket, which indicated that a five-way fight was in prospect. There was also Schumacher's shunt at *Variante Alta* during free practice on Saturday morning, which the *tifosi* seized upon as a signal that the pressure was getting to him.

The weather added a streak of complication, however, for just before the start the sun began to peep through the dark clouds, making the initial tyre choice critical. All five fastest drivers eventually plumped for 'wets', but Mika Hakkinen, sixth on the grid for McLaren-Mercedes, opted for slicks, and so did Mansell and Jordan driver Eddie Irvine.

Schumacher led the pack away, and everyone safely negotiated the new *Tamburello*, giving the lie to fears that it might be the sort of bottleneck one associates with the first corner at Monza. Berger was second, followed by Coulthard and Hill, with Alesi fifth. Those on slicks quickly realized the error of their judgment, and Mansell came in at the end of the lap not only for wets, but also for a new nosecone after touching Gianni Morbidelli's Footwork in *Tamburello*. It was not an auspicious start to what would turn out to be a disastrous comeback for the former World Champion.

After six laps Berger judged that it was dry enough for slicks and he immediately started lapping faster than anyone else. By the time Schumacher had followed suit, the Ferrari had gone by to build up a useful lead, while Hill moved ahead of Coulthard by virtue of a faster pit stop. They, too, were now on slicks.

Schumacher got back into the race in second place, just ahead of Hill, but that lasted only as far as the *Rivazza*. As he crested the hill at the top of the plunge down to the corner where Prost had lost his Ferrari back in 1991, the Benetton snapped from his control and began a frightening high-speed spin after hitting the barriers to the right of the track. Eventually it came to rest in the gravel on the outside of *Rivazza* after what had been a very big accident, leaving the reigning World Champion to walk back to the pits in a thoughtful frame of mind. He was convinced something was amiss with the car, but Benetton found nothing. Most suspected that he had pushed a little bit too hard in tricky conditions in a car which was very unforgiving to drive right on the limit.

The *tifosi*'s joy at Berger's lead lasted until his second tyre and fuel stop on the 22nd lap, when the engine stalled and he lost 27 seconds. Hill sailed by into a lead he would not lose. Coulthard got very close to him, especially after Ukyo Katayama had seriously delayed Hill while being lapped, but then the Scot lost ground behind backmarkers. Then Alesi began to challenge him very seriously, until his next stop.

Coulthard caught up with Hill again, but just when he seemed likely to start pushing for the lead he spun at *Villeneuve*, though a fast recovery and a good tyre and fuel stop would keep him ahead of Alesi so that they could resume their battle for second place. As Coulthard had his hands full, Hill was able to pull comfortably away. The remaining pit stops came and went without drama, but Coulthard was then called in for one of the new 10-second stop-and-go penalties that had been introduced in conjunction with the new speed limit in the pit lane, after his car's automatic speed-limiting device had malfunctioned. This dropped the Scot behind Berger, but he would keep comfortably ahead of Hakkinen and the German Heinz-Harald Frentzen in the Sauber-Ford, who were both lapped.

At one stage Mansell had climbed as high as fifth, but he tangled with Irvine when he failed to see the Ulsterman trying to overtake, and both were delayed further. Irvine needed a new nose, Mansell a fresh right rear tyre. The Jordan driver eventually finished eighth, and Mansell a disgruntled 10th. When the McLaren proved uncompetitive again in the following race, in Barcelona, he retired in anger just after he had been lapped by Schumacher's victorious Benetton. Thereafter his Formula One career, which at times had proved so electrifying – particularly so on occasion at Imola – petered to an unhappy and inglorious end...

Ferrari did not quite achieve the miracle the *tifosi* sought, but Berger was cheerful afterwards after the ever-vociferous and enthusiastic crowd had broken through barriers and scaled safety fences, forcing some drivers to abandon their cars in the pit approach roads. Gerhard was one of them, and he said: "This was perhaps the best atmosphere I can recall in my entire career. If I think back on all those flags and all that emotion, I still get goosepimples. It was a stupendous, incredible experience. Who knows what would have happened if we'd won..."

Alesi was disenchanted, however, and slammed Coulthard's driving in the post-race press conference, accusing him of underhand tactics and dirty tricks. Upon hearing of this, the Scot presented himself at Ferrari and dealt with the matter in such a polite manner that Alesi, who was still letting his adrenalin flow wind down, was completely taken aback. They parted on good terms!

Hill, meanwhile, was delighted with one of the most convincing victories of his short career, and those who witnessed the triumph saw it not only as that, but as a just reward for his bravery in racing the previous year, and for carrying the Williams team forward that season. "As a Grand Prix driver, if you have any understanding of what Ayrton Senna was about, if you have any appreciation of what made him so good, then you know that the best respect you can pay to his memory is to produce the sort of performance which he had always aimed for," he said afterwards. "That would mean total concentration and application, with the single aim of winning."

He grinned sheepishly as he added: "This win is a birthday present for my wife, because I forgot to get her one yesterday..."

But the San Marino Grand Prix was not, he stressed, a sad event, and he was correct when he said that the weekend was not one weighed down by sentimentality. There was, rightly, a great deal of emotion reserved for Senna and Ratzenberger. Many laid flowers at *Tamburello*, and drivers such as Mika Salo of Tyrrell went quietly to pay similar tribute at the spot where his friend Roland had died. And in one of the least publicized feats of tremendous courage, Roland's father Rudolph had made the pilgrimage to the race to honour the memory of his son and, perhaps, to try and make some sense of it all. But the mood of the meeting was one of awareness of the sadness of the previous year, mixed with a determination to take motor racing forward, and to ensure that lessons had been learned.

Perhaps the last word in the story should belong to Patrick Head, not only because of the personal grief he experienced at Imola, but because he is one of the few people within Formula One with a capacity not only to assess immediate problems, but to see beyond them, to the fresh horizons and the disparate tangents that lead from them.

"In my view *Tamburello* was extremely dangerous. I think there had been a number of indications that not much had to go wrong there to cause a car to have a major impact. I say not much, but I mean there had been enough cases of things where drivers had only survived by pure chance. But I don't think that we can just say that it was exclusively Imola's fault. One has to remember that the FIA approved the circuit's safety and that all of the drivers and all of we people in the team, if we had collectively made the point...

"I don't know; there was a funny thing. Whenever your car went past the pits at Imola, we in the Williams team, because of having had two accidents there before, were always aware of the danger at that corner. Or not so much of the corner, but its lack of the appropriate run-off area."

But if it comes to it, the media didn't make a big fuss about that, either. Nobody did. Hard or not, that's the way life is. We learn after events, and sometimes the lessons of our own making can be hard to take. Back in 1979, there had been criticism of the lack of run-off areas, especially at *Tamburello*, but reacting to any suggestion that this had haunted Imola, Peter Gethin made a perfectly valid point when he said: "To be honest, I think that's reading something into that that's possibly true, but is a little dramatic. You can use that about any circuit in the world. If you wanted to you could go to any circuit in the world, that used to run races and that runs races today, and say: 'Why didn't we do this? Why didn't we do that?' You can't say that about just that one circuit. You can say that about all circuits."

"That's the thing," said Head. "We're all to blame for not recognizing something. But to have turned round and exclusively damned the circuit

I think would not really have been appropriate.

"I personally think that Hockenheim is still extremely dangerous. I mean, there you are sitting at 200mph-plus, going down four long straights... You can never say that it's not possible for a gearbox to seize up, that it's not possible for a bit to come off a rear wing, that it's not possible for a suspension component to break when you're going down a straight. Because when you're going down a straight, although the car is running in a straight line it's subjected to enormous loadings on the aerodynamic side. And there you are, with a very narrow track, pretty low Armco, and on the other side of the Armco just a load of trees... Whereas with all these other circuits we're tending to go for very clinical, boring layouts and it's a different safety standard.

"Damon says it's partly exciting at Hockenheim, but that when you're whistling down those straights in those sort of tree tunnels, you breathe a sigh of relief every time your foot comes off the throttle and you're slowing down again.

"When I raise that subject, it's in the light of saying that we all knew that *Tamburello* was dangerous and we didn't do anything about it, but we all know that Hockenheim is dangerous as well. It's one of those things where you have to say: 'What level of danger is considered acceptable at any one time?' It's a moving target."

It's a question, in fact, that has been asked ever since men started racing cars.

WHAT DID HAPPEN TO AYRTON SENNA'S CAR?

Once the enormity of the events of 1994 had begun to sink in, this was the one question everybody was asking. Goodyear ruled out tyre failure, and it seemed unlikely, even though the laps behind the safety car had reduced tyre temperatures and pressures and thus ride heights, that Senna had been thrown off line by a bump. The onboard video evidence clearly shows that he made no attempt to fight the car as it continued on its fatal trajectory.

Much was made later of the sight of the steering column lying by the shattered chassis, having broken at a point where Senna had asked for modification after the Brazilian Grand Prix so he could sit more comfortably in the cockpit. Did the column break? If it did, did it cause the accident, or was the break a result of the impact? Did the power steering then in use malfunction? Why did the team disconnect the power steering mechanism before Hill took the restart?

Such questions ultimately fell to Professor Enrico Lorenzini at Bologna University, who was appointed to head the complex official inquiry into the tragedy demanded under Italian law, and would pass his findings on for further deliberation to Maurizio Passarini, a 37 year-old magistrate in Bologna.

The report was expected too soon, perhaps, but even so there was widespread disbelief when the rumour went round at Christmas time in 1994 that it would not appear before May the following year, for some sort of announcement had keenly been expected around November 30. Then, however, Passarini had asked for more time for further tests.

The precise nature of them has never been revealed, but it is well known that students at the University of Bologna; the founder of Reynard Racing Cars, Adrian Reynard, who was appointed by the Senna family; former Ferrari engineer Mauro Forghieri; former Minardi engineer Tommaso Carletti; former Benetton and Scuderia Italia pilot Emanuele Pirro; former Ferrari and FIA observer Roberto Nosetto; and Dr Rafaele Dalmonte, of the Olympic Committee, have all seen the shattered remains of the Williams FW16B for considerably longer than Williams' Technical Director, Patrick Head, who was permitted some 10 minutes of brief study under a damp awning in the paddock at Imola, and another similar spell later on.

There have been many meetings of experts, but Head has at times expressed concern that simple technical data, specifically expressed in terms that laymen can grasp, has apparently not been understood fully. "We sent some data, and were asked to clarify it," he said in 1995. "I am concerned that what has been said during the period since the accident does not appear to reflect understanding of what we actually said, even though we were asked by the people investigating to couch the revised version in layman's language." Williams itself is forbidden to make any official comment, on the orders of the Senna Foundation.

In the absence of hard information, rumours abounded. The strongest of these, despite Head's insistence and illustrated confirmation that the telemetry continued to show some steering input forces, is that the steering did indeed fail. Telemetry that has been published also indicates an unusual and unaccountable fluctuation in hydraulic pressure in the steering system 12.4 seconds into that final lap.

Why else, it has been suggested, would Senna so instantly have stamped on the brakes that, in the 0.9 seconds before the collision with the wall, he sliced away some 60mph from the 192 that the telemetry said he was achieving through the corner? Why had he left two lines of rubber for the whole 18 metres of track between the point when something went so drastically wrong, and the point of initial impact? Had it been almost any other sort of failure, the instinct would have been to fight the car, to keep the power on and to wrestle delicately with the wheel. But the failure of the mechanism held between the driver's super-sensitive hands would give such instant warning of imminent catastrophe that his immediate reaction would be to kill speed as fast as possible. Others have suggested that he ran over debris from the startline accident, that in some unspecified way caused him to lose control. They point out that his line the previous lap had taken him to the left, over the debris site, whereas Schumacher had kept more to the right along the pit straight.

Of course, this is all pure speculation; informed, perhaps, but speculation nonetheless. Nothing was confirmed either way, and comments attributed to Senna's brother Leonardo only fanned the flames. "Frank Williams told me that the car was hitting the ground more than normal", he told the Brazilian press, adding: "Only a mechanical problem could have caused such a crash." Quite possibly the reduction in tyre temperatures and ride heights could account for the bottoming at this stage, so soon after the restart and before the tyres had resumed their correct temperatures and pressures, but a hungry media instantly seized upon the distraught young man's words and took Williams' comments as an admission. Likewise, a British journalist, who did not understand a technical point that Head made to him on the evening of the accident, mistakenly believed that Patrick had made what amounted to a similar admission. He had not.

Cynics suggested that the Italian authorities wanted to get the 1995 San Marino Grand Prix out of the way before any report was published. But it had still not appeared by the time of the Italian Grand Prix that September. It had not appeared officially by the time this book reached print. As long ago as November 1994, Passarini told Richard Williams of *The Independent on Sunday*: "The problem involves the co-ordination between experts, who are professional people with other responsibilities and obligations. The quality of their analysis is fundamental to the inquiry." He added: "Time is marching on. There's no deadline, but we can't leave the matter for eternity."

Yet still the mystery remained unsolved, complicated by the findings of metallurgists that the steering column showed signs of both metal fatigue and impact damage, and Head's quiet insistence that it would have been impossible to generate any of the telemetry data which confirmed that there had been steering input if the column had already sheared. But then Roberto Causo, the FIA lawyer who was engaged to represent both Williams and Simtek in any possible legal action by the Italian authorities, suggested that the onboard cameras showed Senna dipping his head at the moment when he discovered the problem, as if something in the cockpit had grabbed his attention. He told *Autosport*: "On the in-car video, you normally see the Nacional decal on the lower part of his crash helmet in the mirror, but this time you see his visor – as if he was looking down..." His inference was that Senna was suddenly looking at the steering wheel.

Some, such as Ecclestone, have gone on record to say that what killed Ayrton Senna was the cranial impact of a shattered suspension arm, which was driven through his crash helmet to inflict a fatal head wound. Sid Watkins suggests otherwise, however.

"I have no evidence that anything penetrated his helmet", he said. "I saw the helmet only briefly at the scene – certainly it was cracked or fractured linearly, but I believe that the visor was intact. My best guess is that the right front wheel struck his helmet, and no helmet would have prevented the head injury he suffered from the blunt impact and energy release."

Then, late in December 1995, a year after the first suggestion of significant delay, came another bombshell when *The Sun* newspaper drew heavily on quotes attributed to Lorenzini, to the effect that the steering column was very much to blame. Speaking about the photographs which had shown the column (which he described as a 'rod') lying alongside Senna's shattered Williams, he said: "It had been badly welded together about a third of the way down and couldn't stand the strain of the race. We discovered scratches on the crack in the steering rod. It seemed like the job had been done in a hurry but I can't say how long before the race. Someone had tried to smooth over the join following the welding. I have never seen anything like it.

"I believe the rod was faulty, probably cracked even during the warm-up and moments before the crash only a tiny piece was left connected and therefore the car didn't respond in the bend."

Williams immediately issued a statement which said: 'The comments published today are unofficial. We are currently awaiting Mr Passarini's official report and cannot make any further comment until this has been published.' The team has never denied that the column had been modified, at Senna's request, to make the driving position more comfortable. And the practise of cleaning up a weld is commonplace.

Lorenzini's comments raised not only yet another furore of speculation and expectation, but further controversy when he subsequently claimed to *Autosport* that he had actually made the remarks to the Italian press the previous February, and that they had even then been interpreted as chosen by journalists concerned. Be that as it may, any such comment seemed remarkably intemperate for a man in his position of responsibility.

Moreover, the serious questions that had already been raised about the manner in which this long overdue report had been compiled, came flooding back. There was a fresh tide of unsettled feeling. The delay in publishing the report had long since reached scandalous proportions, though similar instances in the past also revealed the inherent sloth of the Italian system.

Italian law requires identification of those culpable in accidents such as Senna's. Yet on every entry ticket there is that line 'Motor racing is dangerous'. Drivers, more than anyone, understand that. Accidents are part of the risk that they accept, and try to calculate. Serious sentences imposed on anyone held to be responsible would serve no purpose beyond following to the letter a law regarded as dubious by the standards of most other countries. And they would certainly jeopardize the whole future of Grand Prix racing in Italy, where nobody would be prepared to race under such implied threat.

Precisely what caused Williams-Renault FW16/2 to veer into the unforgiving wall at *Tamburello* that day in May 1994 has yet to be identified officially to the satisfaction of all parties concerned. The only certainty is that, whatever emerges when the official report is finally made public, the echoes of Imola will continue to be heard, not only through the hills and terraces surrounding this picturesque and challenging circuit, but throughout the entire world of motor racing, for many years to come.

Index